TEENS ~
OUT = OF = THE = BOX
COPING SKILLS

Facilitator Reproducible Activities for Groups and Individuals

Ester R.A. Leutenberg

Carol Butler, MS Ed, RN, C

Illustrated by
Amy L. Brodsky, LISW-S

wholeperson
Stress & Wellness Publishers
Duluth, Minnesota

wholeperson
Stress & Wellness Publishers

101 W. 2nd St., Suite 203
Duluth, MN 55802

800-247-6789

books@wholeperson.com
www.wholeperson.com

Teens – Out-of-the-Box Coping Skills
Facilitator Reproducible Activities for Groups and Individuals

All efforts have been made to ensure accuracy of the
information contained in this book as of the date published.
The author(s) and the publisher expressly disclaim
responsibility for any adverse effects arising from the use or
application of the information contained herein.

Printed in the United States of America

10 9 8 7 6 5 4 3 2 1

Editorial Director: Carlene Sippola
Art Director: Joy Morgan Dey
Assistant Art Director: Mathew Pa
wlak

Library of Congress Control Number: 2014957798
ISBN: 978-157025-325-6

Why this Book is Entitled "*Teens ~ Out-of-the-Box Coping Skills*"

To introduce the activities in an exciting way, at the start of every session, a teen takes an item from a brightly decorated box and learns the skill of thinking outside-of-the-box in creative ways. This hands-on action and the visual aids foster anticipation, participation and revelation.

Out-of-the-Box Modalities

- Acrostics, cutout puzzles
- Analogies, parables
- Brainstorming
- Bumper stickers, tee shirt slogans
- Cartoons, collages, doodles, drawings, mazes, squiggles, captions
- Charades, dance, pantomime, improvisational theater
- Demonstrations, discussions, guess-the-skill scenarios, presentations
- Flash cards
- Games
- Hidden pictures
- Impersonations
- Interviews
- Media message simulations: ads, blogs, commercials, documentaries, magazine spreads, movie clips, online profiles, overwrites, posts, reality show clips, skits, social media, song lyrics, sports events, replays, texts, videos, voice-overs, websites
- Mind maps
- News broadcasts
- Pass-the-paper
- Posters
- Quotations
- Situation prompts
- Speech balloons, thought bubbles
- Surveys
- Traditional techniques: sentence completion, matching, fill in the blanks
- Writing: poetry, prose, tongue twisters, new word creations, story in six words, storyboard

> Students *"are more like oysters than sausages.*
> *The job of teaching is not to stuff them and then seal them up,*
> *but to help them open and reveal the riches within."*
>
> ~Sydney J. Harris

Format of the Book

Introduction for Teen Participants
This motivates the teens to think outside of the box and engage in activities in creative ways. Suggestion - present the handout as an overview before the first session (page vii).

Cover page for each chapter
The cover page of each chapter describes each of the sessions and provides a pertinent quotation to help facilitators in the following ways:
- Topic selection
- Preparation of group
- Discussion stimulation

This will prompt a creative, out-of-the-box experience for the teens. After the first activity in each chapter, the cover page can be photocopied and distributed to teens to vote on which activity they would like to do next.

The back of each cover page lists the coping skills in each activity.
- Teens can preview the skills they will work on.
- Facilitators may use these as behavioral goals and lists of competencies.

Seven Chapters
1. De-Stress
2. Build Emotional Empowerment
3. Develop Healthy Habits
4. Manage Social Media
5. Stand Up for Self and Others
6. Overcome Obstacles
7. Advance Beyond Coping – Thrive

Information about Chapters
Sessions may stand alone based on specific needs.
Facilitators may skip around; pick and choose among different activities.
A chapter may serve as an entire workshop.
Most handouts adapt to individual or group use.

Components in each session
Reproducible handouts - Facilitators may photocopy and distribute as is or white out and/or add
text as desired and then photocopy.

For the Facilitator - Information on the back of each handout *(For the Facilitator page)*:
  I. **Purpose**
     The goals for the teens in each session.
  II. **General Comments**
     Brief background information.
  III. **Possible Activities**
     Ways to present topics and responses to elicit.
  IV. **Enrichment Activities**
     Additional learning experiences; ways to conclude and follow up.

Coping Skills that Teens will Practice in these Chapters

Chapter Cover Pages

Front: Skills are defined for teens.

Back: Competencies for the facilitators to evaluate.

Throughout all of the chapters, teens will be encouraged to do the following:

Demonstrate oral, written and creative expression skills.

Practice giving and receiving feedback.

1. De-Stress
- Diversions
- Emotional identification, acceptance, empowerment, endurance
- Impulse control
- Perspective, visual and emotional
- Self protection
- Social awareness
- Stress management and stress as a motivator
- Thought changing

2. Build Emotional Empowerment
- Altruism
- Anger management
- Compassion
- Facing fears
- Handling hurt feelings
- Handling temptation
- Humor
- Perseverance
- Self-control
- Selflessness and healthy selfishness
- Positive self-talk
- Reversing apathy

3. Develop Healthy Habits
- Decision making
- Healthy habits
- Positive reinforcement
- Self-change

4. Manage Social Media
- Analysis and interpretation
- Authenticity
- Body image awareness and acceptance
- Handle envy
- Role modeling
- Self-disclosure (as appropriate)
- Social Skills

5. Stand Up for Self and Others
- Advocacy
- Assertiveness
- Courageousness
- Empathy
- Non-judgmental attitude
- Resiliency
- Respect

6. Overcome Obstacles
- Goal setting
- Gratitude
- Inner strength development
- Overcome obstacles
- Possibility thinking
- Problem solving
- Spirituality
- Visualization

7. Advance Beyond Coping – Thrive
- Bravery
- Faith and hope
- Healthy risk taking
- Humanitarianism
- Kindness
- Purposeful life
- Self-challenge, discovery, improvement
- Social consciousness
- Volunteerism

Ideas to Facilitate Innovative Coping Skills

> *Tell me and I forget.*
> *Teach me and I remember.*
> *Involve me and I learn.*
> ~Benjamin Franklin

Teens ~ Out-of-the-Box Coping Skills activities are creative out of the box ways to develop coping skills.

Obtain a box large enough for a magazine or a page printed from the computer. Encourage volunteers to decorate the box to make the sessions even more unusual and fun.

A volunteer takes an item or a picture from the box at the start of each session and shows it to the group to introduce the topic. Tell the teens that the activities pertaining to the box are creative, out-of-the-box ways to learn coping skills.

Tip – keep magazines on hand for illustrations and plan a quick computer search for "a picture of ___."
　　Items suggested for the box are easily accessible. Pictures may be substituted.

Before any session
- Glance at chapter cover pages which summarize each activity.
- Select the handout and review the facilitator information on the back.
- Place the suggested item or picture into the box.
- Decide on the format; often individual, team, board activity or other variations are suggested.
- Photocopy the handouts.
- Select a volunteer to take the item out of the box and show the group.

Teens learn through involvement:
- Put their own spin on quotes or poems.
- Create drawings or symbolizations.
- Portray concepts through charades or improvisations.
- Compose bumper stickers or tee shirt slogans.
- Write texts, poetry and prose.
- Become a game show host or a team player.
- Develop a simulated online *real deal* profile.
- Use other methods of introspective and interactive expression.

Some ground rules to review with teens:
Keep confidentiality – what is said in the sessions stays in the sessions.
Use code names for the privacy of people they write about and themselves.
Example: "MBS" for "My buddy Steve."
Talk with a teacher, counselor or other trusted adult if overwhelming feelings surface in the session.

Facilitators remain vigilant for signs that a teen could endanger self or others, has severe conflict at home, needs to address serious issues, or suffers from emotional or addiction problems, etc.

Refer troubled teens to a school counselor, mental health or medical professional; if danger is imminent, call 911 or the local emergency services number or arrange for teens to go to the nearest hospital emergency department.

Introduction for Teen Participants

If you already *think outside the box*
or
If you want to tap into your creative side
or
If you'd like to learn skills to handle your issues …

These activities are for you!

Through the activities in *Teens ~ Out-of-the-Box Coping Skills* you'll figure out ways to grow:
Cope with stress
Empower yourself
Develop Healthy Habits
Manage Social Media
Stand Up for Your Self and Others
Overcome Obstacles
Go Beyond Coping – to Thrive!

**Would you rather be a sausage, crammed full of facts about skills?
Or an oyster, discovering your inner pearls of insight?**

To discover YOUR insights …
Express your ideas, concerns, hopes and dreams.
Invent new ways to think, feel, react and act.
Keep your discoveries private or choose to share.

Above all, be an oyster!

Reflect, ask questions, give opinions and receive feedback; draw, write, act, play games;
be a leader or a team member; create posters, bumper stickers or tee shirt slogans;
and participate in many opportunities.

You may decide, as did Maya Angelou …

*My mission in life is not to merely survive, but to thrive;
and to do so with some passion,
some compassion, some humor, and some style.*

Teens ~ Out-of-the-Box Coping Skills

TABLE OF CONTENTS

(Continued on the next page)

Teens ~ Out-of-the-Box Coping Skills

TABLE OF CONTENTS *(continued)*

(Continued on the next page)

© 2015 WHOLE PERSON ASSOCIATES, 101 W. 2ND ST., SUITE 203, DULUTH MN 55802 • 800-247-6789

Teens ~ Out-of-the-Box Coping Skills

TABLE OF CONTENTS *(continued)*

Deepest Gratitude to ...

our teen reviewer Hannah Lavoie

and the professionals who make us look good ...

Editor and Lifelong Teacher – Eileen Regen, M.Ed., CJE

Illustrator – Amy L. Brodsky, LISW-S

Art Director – Joy Dey

Assistant Art Director – Mathew Pawlak

Editorial Director – Carlene Sippola

Proofreader – Jay Leutenberg

DE-STRESS ①

Stress should be a powerful driving force, not an obstacle.

~ Bill Phillips

Chapter 1 - De-Stress Behavioral Coping Skills

Throughout the chapter, teens will communicate through oral, written and creative expression and give and receive feedback.

Teens: Skills in each activity.
Facilitators: Competencies to evaluate.

Step Back for the Whole Picture
- Illustrate a visual perspective about a situation.
- Describe an emotional perspective about a situation.
- State the main thought about the situation.
- Identify feelings about the situation.
- Explain the difference between what acceptance is and is not.
- Identify relaxation techniques to use to reduce anxiety.

Waves of Emotions
- Express emotions.
- Identify ways to do what one needs to do, despite fear.
- State ways to bravely handle a setback.
- Explain ways challenges can be exciting.

Do the Opposite
- Describe ways to do the opposite of a first impulse in times of stress.
- State in which situations it is better to let instincts be the guide.
- Identify actions to take, despite fear, while expecting calmer feelings to follow.
- Name circumstances in which additional action is needed beyond doing the opposite.

Choose Your Distress or Eustress Train
- State thoughts that lead to destructive stress.
- Share thoughts that use stress as a motivator.
- Practice changing thoughts to identify where *possibility thinking* leads.
- Describe a potential inner bully.
- Identify an inner troublemaker and thoughts that fight against each other.
- Quote positive thoughts that would guide a person.

Put on Protective Gear
- Identify potentially painful words people could use to hurt others.
- Describe non-verbal unkind acts people could direct toward others.
- Demonstrate emotional self-defense techniques against cruelty.
- State the possible motivations of people who mistreat others.

Develop Diversions
- Demonstrate enjoyable diversions that reduce stress.
- Name the pros and cons of diversions.
- Identify sources of help for issues that need more assistance than diversions alone.
- Practice problem-solving skills.

A Stress-Less Kit
- Identify unhelpful quick-fixes for stress.
- State effective techniques to handle stress.
- Compose stress-buster messages.
- Find words of wisdom about converting stress from negative to positive.
- Create quotations to handle stress.

Step Back for the Whole Picture

My stressful situation looks like this close up

Like a camera zooms in for a close-up, you may focus too intensely on one stressful aspect of your situation.
Imagine that you mentally step back, breathe deeply, and see the whole picture.

My stressful situation looks like this from a distance

My main thought is …

_____

My main feeling is …

_____

I realize …

My thought is a stream of words.
My feeling is a passing sensation.
I do not judge or try to change my reaction now.
I accept that "It is what it is."

Step Back for the Whole Picture

FOR THE FACILITATOR

I. Purpose

To cope with a distressing event through perspective, attention to reactions and acceptance.
To express what is seen and felt without becoming angry or overwhelmed, or running or hiding.

II. General Comments

Initially in a crisis, stepping back, breathing and focusing help teens accept a current reality (Ideally, teens will later reframe thoughts with resultant changes in feelings and actions).

III. Possible Activities

a. Before the session, place a camera or cell phone, or a picture of a camera or cell phone, into the box.
b. At the start of the session, a volunteer takes the item out of the box and shows it to the group.
c. Ask the purpose of close-ups (to see details well).
d. Ask the disadvantages of close-ups (they show only a small segment of a scene).
e. Ask the advantage of stepping back when taking a photo (to capture the whole picture).
f. Distribute the *Step Back for the Whole Picture* handout; a volunteer reads text at the top aloud.
g. Ask how it helps to mentally step back (to see the whole situation); the perceived crisis may really be a small blip; a truly unfortunate circumstance may have hidden blessings.
h. Direct teens to draw a close-up and a distant view of a current stressful situation and complete the sentences at the bottom of the page.
i. Allow time for completion.
j. Ask about the advantage of seeing thoughts as streams of words and feelings as passing sensations.
Elicit that this decreases their intensity and allows teens to express what they see and feel without being overwhelmed, or needing to run or hide.
k. Encourage teens to share their responses and receive peer feedback.
l. Ask "Why not judge the situation or your reactions?" (non-productive, self-defeating).
m. Ask "Why not try to change the situation or your reactions? (accept the moment as it is; change what can be changed later).
n. Write "What acceptance is NOT" on the board; ask teens to brainstorm.
   Possibilities
   Acceptance is NOT:
   • Approval of the situation.
   • Permission for the situation to continue.
   • Proof that one's perception of the event is factual.
   • Avoidance of change in a situation or to a reaction.
o. Ask teens the value of focusing on one's thoughts and feelings at the very moment of distress.
Elicit that it prevents added worries about the past or future.

IV. Enrichment Activities

a. Encourage teens to describe more details about their recent distressing events:
   • Physical sensations
   • Sights
   • Sounds
b. Ask how it will help teens in the future to stand back, breathe and focus:
   • Stay in the moment.
   • Slow down racing thoughts.
   • Avoid value judgments; labeling events as "terrible" or feelings as "bad" worsens them.

Waves of Emotions

"You can't stop the waves, but you can learn to surf." ~ Kabat-Zinn

(In the box below, draw a surfer on a surfboard with waves all around.)

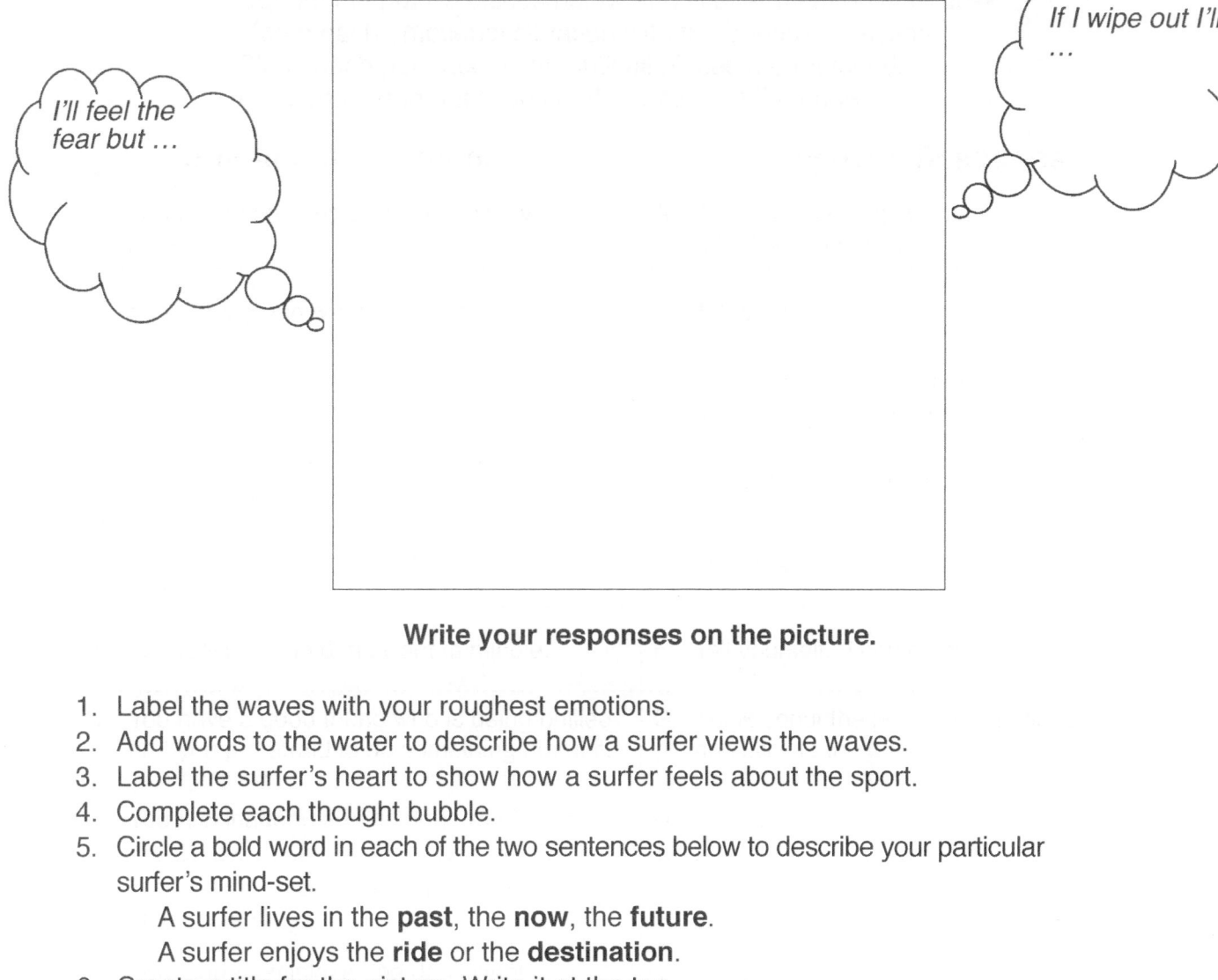

I'll feel the fear but …

If I wipe out I'll …

Write your responses on the picture.

1. Label the waves with your roughest emotions.
2. Add words to the water to describe how a surfer views the waves.
3. Label the surfer's heart to show how a surfer feels about the sport.
4. Complete each thought bubble.
5. Circle a bold word in each of the two sentences below to describe your particular surfer's mind-set.

    A surfer lives in the **past**, the **now**, the **future**.

    A surfer enjoys the **ride** or the **destination**.
6. Create a title for the picture. Write it at the top.
7. Write the caption "I will sometimes need to eat some sand" below your picture.
8. How does this caption relate to your life?

_____

_____

_____

_____

Waves of Emotions

FOR THE FACILITATOR

I. Purpose
To experience emotions and embrace challenges; to develop a surfer mindset.

II. General Comments
Teens may try to suppress or intensify emotions they perceive as unpleasant.

III. Possible Activities
a. Before the session, place a drawing or picture of waves into the box.
b. At the start of the session, a volunteer takes the item out of the box and shows it to the group.
c. Ask the group how waves resemble emotions (powerful, changeable, unpredictable; can be thrilling
and exhilarating; may be dangerous).
d. Encourage teens to share experiences or knowledge about surfing.
e. Distribute the *Waves of Emotions* handout; a volunteer reads aloud the title and quotation on the top of the page.
f. Allow time for completion.
g. Encourage teens to share responses and receive peer feedback.
Possibilities corresponding to the handout's numbers
1. Rough emotions may be fear, stress, sadness, jealousy, anger, inferiority, etc.
2. Surfers view waves as possibly scary, challenging, exciting, and essential.
3. Surfers feel passion, fire, love for the sport (despite or because of its ups and downs).
4. Thought bubbles:
    "I'll feel the fear but … ride the wave," etc.
    "If I wipe out … I'll get back on the board," etc.
5. Word choices – now; ride.
6. Individualized titles, e.g., Ride the Waves, Feel and Deal, etc.
7. "I will sometimes need to eat some sand" will be written as a caption.
8. The caption helps teens recognize that setbacks are part of life and learning.

IV. Enrichment Activities
Encourage teens to brainstorm aspects of a surfer's mindset that apply to life; a teen lists ideas on board.
Possibilities
- Gain knowledge about the ocean (learn about thoughts, emotions, situations to be faced).
- It's ok to be a beginner (start right now to embrace emotions).
- Be prepared with the right board, wetsuit, etc. (have coping skills ready to deal with anything).
- Manage risks sensibly, honor posted warnings, etc. (avoid real dangers but take healthy risks).
- Help a surfer in trouble or one who needs pointers (care about people, share your knowledge).
- Don't surf alone (develop a support system).
- Signal when in trouble (ask for help before the problem becomes unmanageable).
- Be one's own cheerleader (praise oneself for dealing with changes and challenges).
- Be patient during flat spells (there will be quiet or unexciting times in life).
- Don't fight the riptide and drown from exhaustion; focus on staying afloat (accept what cannot be changed and use coping skills to rise above or make the best of turbulent times).

DO THE OPPOSITE

Newton's Third Law of Motion states "For every action there is an equal and opposite reaction."
The same applies to feelings – for every emotion there is an equal and opposite reaction.
Often, to do the opposite of what you want to do at the moment is the better way to cope.

Example: When angry, the impulse is to punch; the better choice is to walk away.
Cut out the puzzle pieces below and scatter them on your desk.
Match each emotional situation with the opposite reaction.
Place each pair face down until all pieces are matched.
Respond to the questions at the bottom of the page.

Emotional Situations	Opposite Reactions
1. You feel depressed and want to stay in bed.	A. State your feelings with an "I feel statement …"
2. You argued and want to hold a grudge.	B. Tell a trusted adult.
3. You lost and want to put down the winner.	C. Smile, and when someone smiles back, strike up a conversation.
4. You were disrespected and want to insult the person.	D. Admit it and apologize.
5. You are afraid and don't want to give a speech.	E. Get up and go out.
6. You feel shy and don't want to mingle.	F. Tell yourself, "I can do it!"
7. You have a good friend who is being bullied and you are afraid to do something about it.	G. Think about the possible consequences and stick to the rules.
8. You feel inadequate and don't want to try.	H. Let it go.
9. You feel invincible and want to drive recklessly.	I. Take a deep breath and step up to the podium.
10. You made a mistake and don't want anyone to know.	J. Say "congratulations" like you mean it.

What emotional situation do you face? _____

What would be your opposite reaction? _____

_____

In what situation would it be better to act on your instincts than to do the opposite? _____

_____

DO THE OPPOSITE
FOR THE FACILITATOR

I. Purpose
To learn that in many situations to do the opposite of one's first impulse is the better way to cope.

II. General Comments
Teens who have developed destructive patterns may benefit from taking the opposite actions.

III. Possible Activities
a. Before the session, decide whether to present the activity as a game, puzzle or matching exercise.
b. Make the specified number of copies and cut or supply scissors as directed for each format below.

Introduction for all formats
c. Before the session, place a book into the box and recruit a volunteer to perform a demonstration.
d. At the start of the session, whisper to the volunteer to retrieve the book from the box and drop it onto the floor.
e. Ask teens what was demonstrated (gravity).
f. Explain that teens will apply a law of physics to emotions.

Game Format
- Photocopy one of the *Do the Opposite* handout and cut on the broken lines.
- Give ten teens a numbered cutout and ten teens a lettered cutout.
- If you have more than twenty teens, some will observe.
- If you have fewer than twenty, give people more than one cutout so all cutouts are used.
- Teens move around and find the person(s) with the matching situation or opposite reaction.
- Pairs then share their situations and reactions with the group.

Individual Puzzle Format
- Make copies for all teens and have several pairs of scissors available.
- Distribute the *Do the Opposite* handout; a volunteer reads the text at the top of the page aloud.
- Teens cut their pages on the broken lines and then match situations with opposite reactions.
- Teens share their responses.

Traditional Matching Exercise
- Make copies for all teens; do not cut the boxes; teens write the correct letter under each number.

Answer Key for all formats: 1–E, 2–H, 3–J, 4–A, 5–I, 6–C, 7–B, 8–F, 9–G, 10–D.

Expect a variety of individual responses for the three questions at the bottom of the page.
g. Emphasize discretion – Know when to take the opposite action and when to "go with your gut."
h. Ask teens about situations in which acting on their instincts or first impulses would be best.

Possibilities
- Someone makes unwanted sexual advances – steer clear.
- A walking route looks deserted – find a more populated path.
- You suspect a scam – don't buy.
- A friend is drinking and about to drive – don't get into the car.
- You sense that a peer wants to harm self or others – tell a trusted adult.

IV. Enrichment Activities
a. Introduce the concept of "just do it!" and positive feelings will follow. Do something that is feared (public speaking, etc.) several times and the fear will decrease.
b. Ask teens to share times they acted the opposite of their feelings and how their emotions changed.
c. Emphasize that doing the opposite may be just the first step in more complex circumstances. In the heat of anger walk away, but after the cool off, conflict resolution may still be needed.

Choose Your Distress or Eustress Train

Picture yourself watching two trains about to leave the station, one train going one way, the other going the opposite way. You need to make a decision as to which train to go on.

In the box below, draw a train with four or five windows, each large enough for a few words. Label each window with one of your thoughts that leads to distress. Example: *I'll fail the test.* Add a destination sign saying "Stress City" to the front of the train.

In the box below, draw the same type of train, however, traveling the other way.
Label each window with one of your thoughts that leads to eustress (stress that helps and motivates you.)
Examples: I'm busy but I'll study my best. - I want to plan my responses for my upcoming interview.
Add a destination sign saying "Peace Park" to the front of the train.

Place an "X" on the train you do not want to hop onto.
Circle the train you choose.

Choose Your Distress or Eustress Train

FOR THE FACILITATOR

I. Purpose
To visualize one's thoughts passing by on trains; to use stress for positive purposes.

II. General Comments
Teens will recognize that thoughts can carry them to destructive or productive destinations.

III. Possible Activities
    a. Before the session, ask a teen to sketch a train; place the picture into the box.
    b. At the start of the session, a volunteer takes the picture out of the box and shows it to the group.
    c. Ask the group why people take trains (to go places).
    d. Ask how thoughts are like trains (they take us places mentally).
    e. Distribute the *Choose Your Distress or Eustress Train* handout; a volunteer reads the text and directions aloud.
    f. Allow time for completion; remind teens that artistic ability and perfect spelling are not important in this handout.
    g. Encourage teens to share their responses and receive peer feedback.
    Possibilities
    Thoughts that lead to distress:
- School is terrible.
- No one likes me.
- I should be like everyone else.
- I'll never have a partner.

    Thoughts that lead to eustress:
- School is what I make of it.
- I like myself.
- I am unique.
- I'm ok with or without a partner.

    h. Encourage teens to see the distress-bound train as an internal bully.
    i. Ask teens to brainstorm ways a person might mentally bully oneself.
    Possibilities:
- Negative self-talk by name calling.
- Magnifying one's own weaknesses and others' strengths.
- Catastrophizing about the worst possible outcome.
- Thinking one knows what others are thinking.
- Caring too much about people's negative opinions.
- Mentally revisiting past misery; predicting it will recur.

IV. Enrichment Activities
    a. Ask teens to visualize themselves as train conductors and then visualize their thoughts as passengers.
    b. Encourage teens to share responses to the following:
- What is your *troublemaker* thought that you need to throw off your train?
- Which two thoughts are fighting with each other?
- What thought will you put in your driver's (engineer's) seat?

    c. Adapt the topic as needed, e.g., the thought trains could be leading to addiction (*example: I need a drink.*) or to recovery (*I need to talk to a supportive person before I mess up and take a drink.*)

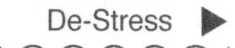

Put on Protective Gear

You cannot control what comes out of someone's mouth.

Draw a stick figure coughing at you. Label their germs with their hurtful words.	Draw yourself wearing a spacesuit to protect against their emotional *germ warfare*.

Your invisible protective gear ...

1. How does it help to know that people spout out their own *emotional germs*?

    _____

    _____

2. What thoughts separate you from others' *emotional germs*?

    _____

    _____

3. What positive actions protect you from the words of *emotional germ warfare*?

    _____

    _____

Put on Protective Gear
FOR THE FACILITATOR

I. Purpose
To inoculate oneself from the stress of cruelty; to know that the negativity stems from the perpetrator's problems and need not harm the intended target.

II. General Comments
Teens are vulnerable to stress caused by people who bully, unkind remarks made by friends, words that wound loved ones.

III. Possible Activities
a. Before the session, place a facial tissue into the box.
b. At the start of the session, a volunteer takes the tissue out of the box and shows it to the group.
c. Ask the purpose of the tissue for people who are coughing (to prevent the spread of germs).
d. Ask "What else that is nasty comes out of mouths?" (words).
e. Ask "How can we protect ourselves from insults?" (ignore them, positive self-talk, etc.).
f. Prompt teens to recall hurtful words someone once said to them or words that could cut deeply.
g. Distribute the *Put on Protective Gear* handout; a volunteer reads the top text and directions aloud.
h. Allow time for completion; remind teens that artistic ability and perfect spelling are not important with this handout.
i. Drawings and the hurtful words will be individualized, e.g., "You are a loser."
j. Encourage teens to share their pictures and responses.
   Possibilities
   1. It helps to know that when people spout out their own emotional germs, cruel comments reflect what's going on inside of them; dissatisfaction with themselves is projected onto others. Many people are infected with false arrogance.
   2. Examples of thoughts that separate:
      I will not take it personally.
      I know the truth about me.
      I can hear with my ears and not take it to heart.
   3. Examples of actions that protect:
      Walk away.
      Ask the person to stop the verbal abuse.
      Tell a trusted adult if anyone is bullying.

IV. Enrichment Activities
a. Ask teens to brainstorm ways people hurt others without using words.
   Possibilities
   • Body language – closed arms, turning away.
   • Exclusion – ignoring a person, not making room in a conversation circle or at a lunch table.
   • Facial expression – rolled eyes, frowns, smirks, dirty looks.
   • Violation of privacy – putting pictures on social media without permission.
   • Other – whispers, giggles, stares, pointed fingers.
b. Encourage teens to share ways to cope with non-verbal cruelty.
   Possibilities
   • Understand that non-verbal insults come from a deficit within the perpetrator.
   • Recognize that when one's basic need for belonging has been thwarted, it does hurt at first.
   • Realize it is impossible to please all people all the time.
   • Live within one's own belief system; honor one's own values.
   • Consider what is important to loved ones if it is in line with one's own best interests.
   • Seek a support system of people who accept and appreciate others' unique qualities.

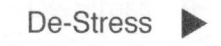

Develop Diversions

Charades

Mind Do puzzles	**Place** Concert	**Creativity** Sculpt
Mind Watch television	**Place** Movie	**Body** Exercise
Mind Play comptuer games	**Creativity** Paint	**Volunteerism** Donate clothes
Mind Read	**Creativity** Write	**Volunteerism** Serve at a food kitchen
Mind Listen to music	**Creativity** Compose a song	**Spiritual** Meditate
Spiritual Smell flowers or scented candles	**Creativity** Play a musical instrument	**Body** Deep breathe
Social Call or text	**Body** Dance	**Body** Muscle relaxation
Place House of worship	**Body** Sing	**Social** Pet an animal
Place Zoo	**Body** Take a walk	**Social** Support group

23

Develop Diversions
FOR THE FACILITATOR

I. **Purpose**
To recall healthy activities that distract from distress.

II. **General Comments**
Teens play charades to portray diversions; teens experientially learn that interactive games relieve stress.

III. **Possible Activities**
   a. Before the session, photocopy the *Develop Diversions* handout and cut on the broken lines.
   b. Place cutouts in a pile face down at the front of the room.
   c. Before the session, place a cell phone or a picture of a cell phone into the box.
   d. At the start of the session, a volunteer takes the item out of the box and shows it to the group.
   e. Ask its purpose (communication, information, entertainment and other diversions).
   f. Ask "What are examples of unhealthy ways to handle stress?" (drink alcohol, use drugs, blame others).
   g. Write Diversions on the board and ask its meaning (ways to be distracted and to relax).
   h. Explain that teens will play charades about stress-reducing diversions.
   i. Teens will take turns picking up a cutout and reading the bold category aloud:
   - Mind
   - Body
   - Social
   - Place
   - Creativity
   - Volunteerism (compassion, charity)
   - Spiritual
   j. Teens then use non-verbal communication to portray the activity.
   k. The person who guesses takes the next turn or calls on someone whose hand is raised.
   l. Most activities can be shown by one player's body language.
   m. A few require helpers, e.g., *Support group* where players may sit in a circle and pretend to talk.
   n. After all cutouts are used, encourage teens to brainstorm other healthy distractions.
   o. Ask "Are diversions always the best way to deal with distress?" (no).
   p. Question teens about the pros of diversions (short term –relax and get some distance from an issue).
   q. Prompt teens to consider the cons (if used excessively they may prevent problem-solving efforts).

IV. **Enrichment Activities**
Encourage teens to identify ways to resolve issues that need more intense interventions.
   Possibilities
   - Talk with a trusted adult.
   - See a medical professional.
   - Ask a teacher or counselor about resources.
   - Seek spiritual or therapist, counselor, etc., support for personal and family issues.
   - Check trusted online information and support (well established governmental guides).
   - Use problem-solving skills – write the issue, brainstorm options, evaluate the pros and cons, etc.

A Stress-Less Kit: Quick Fixes that are Quacks

Create a list to remind yourself and others what NOT to do in times of stress.

A quack is a con artist, a fake.
Some behaviors seem helpful at the time, but they hurt in the long run.
Example: Alcohol poses as your friend to relieve stress for the moment.
Afterward, the problem remains, plus you have a hangover.
You may have other results such as causing an accident that harms someone.

Make your own list of quacky quick fixes:

1.

2.

3.

4.

5.

6.

7.

8.

9.

10.

25

A Stress-Less Kit: What Works? Posters

Create posters to help yourself and others in times of stress.

Convey your message through stick figures, cartoons, caricatures, symbols, collages, etc.
Feel free to add thought or speech bubbles and/or captions.

Think about what works for you in times of stress:

Handle the issue in a positive way.
Use stress productively.
Recall what calms you.
Remember what motivates you.
(Example: A person on a nature walk.)

A Stress-Less Kit: Stress-Less Slogans

Compose stress-buster slogans to help yourself and others.

Catchy slogans may be used on tee shirts or bumper stickers.
(Example: Stress is the spice of life.)

Cut out your favorite slogans.
Keep them with you to de-stress.

A Stress-Less Kit: Ace an Acrostic

Develop a few acrostics to help yourself and others in times of stress.

This type of acrostic puzzle/poem uses the first letter of each line to form a word to begin a statement.

Example: **CRISIS**

C – *Chill out with time-out.*
R – *Recognize inner strength.*
I – *Involve trusted people.*
S – *Seek spiritual support.*
I – *Investigate all options.*
S – *See benefits in the challenge.*

A Stress-Less Kit: Quotations

Research and copy quotations, or create your own, to help yourself and others to conquer a crisis.

Find words of wisdom from others or tap into your "Inner Guru."

Example: Adopting the right attitude can convert a negative stress into a positive one.

~ Hans Selye

Quotable Quotes

1.

2.

3.

4.

5.

6.

7.

8.

9.

10.

A Stress-Less Kit

FOR THE FACILITATOR

I. Purpose
To decide what does and does not work to reduce or to use stress productively.

II. General Comments
Teens collaborate to cope with stress by developing an emergency kit.

III. Possible Activities
a. The *A Stress-Less Kit* five handouts can be used with individuals or groups in one or five sessions.
b. Before the session, decide which option to use and make photocopies of the page(s) to be distributed.
c. Before the session, place a first-aid kit, or a picture of a first-aid kit, into the box.
d. At the start of the session, a volunteer takes the item out of the box and shows it to the group.
e. Ask teens, "What is the purpose of a first-aid kit?" (To handle injuries or minor medical emergencies.)
f. Ask teens, "When would an emotional first-aid kit be needed?" (When someone is feeling anxious or in distress).
g. Explain that teens will develop a stress-less kit for group members to use when needed.
h. Emphasize that artistic ability and perfect spelling are not needed with this handout; focus on the message.
i. For those teens who agree, projects will be photocopied and then distributed, saved in backpacks, notebooks, etc.

Individual Format, five sessions
- Distribute the exact same handout to each teen for five different sessions.
- Allow time for completion. Encourage teens to share their responses and receive peer feedback.

Individual Format, one session
- Write the titles and types of activities on the board:
  Quick Fixes that are Quacks (lists)
  What Works? (posters)
  Stress Less (slogans)
  Ace an Acrostic (word puzzle)
  Quotations (find or formulate)
- Each teen selects a handout based on activity preference.
- Allow time for completion. Encourage teens to share their work and receive peer feedback.

Team Format, five sessions
- Distribute the exact same handout to each teen for five different sessions.
- Each team completes one project; for posters, teens add to a drawing or give ideas for art and text.
- The group re-convenes; teams share their work and receive feedback from other teams.

Team Format, one session
- Write the titles and types of activities on the board (see "Individual Format, one session" above).
- Allow teens to choose their projects and join teammates with the same preference.
- Each team completes one project; for posters, teens add to a drawing or give ideas for art and text.
- The group re-convenes; teams share their work and receive feedback from other teams.

For all formats
- Photocopy the completed handouts and distribute to teens for their Stress-Less Kits.

IV. Enrichment Activities
- Suggest that teens decorate a Stress-Less Kit box and/or portable project folder, take photos of posters to save in their cell phones, and transfer lists, slogans and acrostics to computerized devices.
- Remind teens that they will have stress management skills at their fingertips.

BUILDING EMOTIONAL EMPOWERMENT

*I don't want to be at the mercy of my emotions.
I want to use them, to enjoy them, and to dominate them.*

~ Oscar Wilde

Chapter 2 – Build Emotional Empowerment Behavioral Coping Skills

Throughout the chapter, teens will communicate through oral, written and creative expression and give and receive feedback.

Teens: Skills in each activity.
Facilitators: Competencies to evaluate.

Anger Flash Cards
- Identify feelings that fuel anger.
- State ways to cope with anger.
- Practice assertive statements.
- Describe traits in people that can heighten angry responses.
- Identify situations that are reminders of past issues and that can spark anger.

Human-i-text-tarian
- Identify possible motivations for people who perpetrate hate crimes.
- State connections to others.
- Suggest ways that caring can be taught in homes, schools and communities.
- Describe ways to play a compassionate role in humanitarian solutions.

Outwit Your Fears
- Use humor to describe fears.
- Share ways to visualize oneself coping positively with a stressful situation.
- State ways to reward oneself for facing challenges.
- Plan ways to gradually become de-sensitized to stressful situations.

Got Grit?
- Give an example of being determined and compare it to giving up.
- Identify actions that will help a person stick to a current task despite difficulties.

Self-ish-less
- Define healthy selfishness or the made-up word self-ish-less.
- State ways to balance others' demands with one's priorities.

Hurt Feelings
- Identify types of outside events that bring out unpleasant feelings.
- State the differences between responses that soothe or worsen hurt feelings.
- Describe actions that could potentially hurt other people's feelings.

Improv – Are You Tempted?
- Describe types of temptation one may encounter.
- Practice ways to handle temptations.
- Identify ways to avoid tempting others.

Self-Talk Tech
- Replace negative self-talk with positive but realistic statements.
- Give examples of self-defeating mindsets.
- Identify steps to reverse self-defeating ideas.

Apathy's Masks
- Reveal possible feelings underneath an "I don't care" attitude.
- Identify the advantages of sharing genuine feelings in the appropriate situations.
- State ways to alleviate apathy.

Anger Flash Cards

Cut out each card. Fold back down the middle and glue or tape the sides together.

✂ **Card #1**

SITUATION	RESPONSE
	1. What feelings, actions and/or words in the situation fuel the anger?
	2. How can you calm down?
	3. What will be your assertive words?

✂ **Card #2**

SITUATION	RESPONSE
	1. What trait do you see in this person that you dislike in yourself or in someone close to you?
	2. What past hurts are surfacing?

Anger Flash Cards

FOR THE FACILITATOR

I. Purpose
To develop insight about, and cope with anger.

II. General Comments
Teens create situational flash cards; then compare their own responses with peers' opinions.

III. Possible Activities
a. Before the session, obtain scissors and tape or glue-stick for participants.
b. Before the session, make a simple math flash card on paper and place into the box.
c. At the start of the session, a volunteer takes the flash card out of the box and shows it to the group.
d. Ask the purpose of flash cards (to help people learn).
e. Explain teens will use their real life experiences with anger to create flash cards.
f. Distribute the *Anger Flash Cards* handout with scissors and glue or tape.
g. Teens cut across tops and bottoms of cards; fold back the middle and glue or tape sides together.
h. Direct teens to do the following:
   - Print their anger-evoking situations on the fronts, e.g., PARTNER FLIRTS.
   - Print words in capital letters and in large print.
   - Write their responses to the questions on the back.
   - Remind teens to use name codes.
i. Teens take turns at the front of the room and hold up their cards; volunteers read the situations. If peers cannot see the print clearly, the writers read their situations aloud.
j. While writers display the front of the card, they read the questions (not responses) on the back aloud.
k. Volunteers respond as they would feel, speak, act etc., in that same situation.
l. The persons who wrote the flash cards then reveal their responses.
m. The audience does NOT make value judgments about the responses but does give feedback about the similarities and differences between the writers' and volunteers' reactions.
n. Continue until all flash cards have been discussed.
o. If not mentioned by teens elicit concepts below:
   Card #1
   1. Feelings, actions or words in this situation – fear of abandonment, embarrassment, powerlessness; guilt; pain, jealousy; aggressive actions; blaming or threatening words, etc.
   2. Calm down – take time out, deep breathe, exercise, tune into what the body is experiencing.
   3. Assertive words – "I feel", "I need", "I will", "I will not", "would you please", "no."
   Card #2
   1. Traits seen in the person will be individualized.
   2. Past hurts, disappointments, unresolved issues, etc. will be personalized.

IV. Enrichment Activities
Encourage teens to brainstorm anger-related concepts; a peer lists their ideas on the board.
   Possibilities
   - Pick your battles – decide what is really important; let the little stuff go.
   - Forgive – for your own sake and for the relationship, if it is valued.
   - Do not demand fairness, appreciation, agreement or your own way.
   - Recognize that a different opinion is not a put down; do not take it personally.
   - Remember that aggression is not a sign of power but of lack of control over oneself.
   - Learn the art of compromise.
   - Agree to disagree.

Human-i-text-tarian

Television Journalist's News Clip

"Today we're talking about hate crimes.
Send your opinions and we'll post your comments on air."

What do you imagine the background of the perpetrators of hate crimes to be?

What do you imagine is in the mind of perpetrators of hate crimes?

Television Journalist's News Clip

"We were flooded with responses to yesterday's question.
Today we're challenging all humanitarians to find solutions.
Text your ideas and you'll be entered into a drawing for the…
Human-i-text-tarian of the Year Award."

In what ways are we all connected?

How can caring for one another be taught instead of hate?

In homes?

In schools?

In society?

Human-i-text-tarian

FOR THE FACILITATOR

I. Purpose
To undermine hate through awareness, connectedness and caring for one another.

II. General Comments
Hate ranges from bullying to killings; hate groups threaten campuses, communities and countries.

III. Possible Activities
a. Before the session, recruit a volunteer to play a news broadcaster; allow the teen to preview the handout.
b. Before the session, place a newspaper or a picture of a newspaper in the box.
c. At the start of the session, a volunteer takes the newspaper out of the box and shows it to the group.
d. Ask about the difference between television news forty years ago and today (it was one way communication; now viewers can connect with broadcasters and each other.)
e. Explain that teens will watch a simulated news clip and then respond through simulated emails or texts.
f. The volunteer goes to the front of the room, portrays a newsperson, and reads the two news clips aloud (the italicized text inside the quotation marks, not the questions).
g. Distribute the Human-i-text-tarian handout; point out the questions and boxes for teens' replies.
h. Allow time for completion.
i. Encourage teens to share their responses and receive peer feedback.
   Possibilities
   - Background and mindset of perpetrators of hate crimes:
     A possible history of being abused and feeling powerless; attempts to compensate for feeling "less than" by putting others down; may blame a minority for all their problems; may belong to a group of haters and want the thrill of bragging about hurting others.
   - Ways we are all connected:
     Physically all people experience cold, hunger, pain; we can give and receive blood and organs from each other.
     Emotionally all people want caring and belonging; we laugh and cry, are moved by the arts and words.
     Intellectually all people strive to understand; we struggle with some situations and are skilled in others.
   - Ways caring can be taught at home:
     Role models embrace diversity rather than promoting prejudice; people show affection, appreciation, honesty and forgiveness.
   - Ways caring can be taught in schools:
     Inclusion programs, anti-bullying campaigns, random acts of kindness, activities in which students talk about how they would want to be treated in certain situations.
   - Ways caring can be taught in society:
     Volunteerism, starting charities, social and political activism.

IV. Enrichment Activities
a. Encourage teens to research anti-hate organizations e.g., The Anti-Defamation League, National Urban League, United Nations World Conference against Racism, etc.
b. Prompt teens to survey peers' opinions about people with unmet needs in their community, country or the world who would benefit from public awareness campaigns or fund-raisers.
c. Suggest that teens become involved in the above noted organizations and activities or other humanitarian efforts.

Outwit Your Fears

Facilitators – please cut out the boxes below and then photocopy the remainder of the page.

Autophobia Fear of being alone or of oneself.	**Bibliophobia** Fear of books.	**Decidophobia** Fear of making decisions.	**Disposaphobia** Fear of throwing things out.	**Glossophobia** Fear of public speaking.
Ideophobia Fear of ideas.	**Neophobia** Fear of anything new.	**Scolionophobia** Fear of school.	**Sociophobia** Fear of society or people.	**Testophobia** Fear of tests.

Outwit Your Fears

Create your own phobia word to describe your own most troublesome fear. _____

You have probably been told "Don't catastrophize," but for this exercise, exaggerate the consequences. It's okay to use humor and have fun!
Ex: If I ask someone out and am turned down I'll NEVER date anybody and be a hermit FOREVER.

_____

_____

_____

Pretend you already coped with the challenge and describe what you did.

_____

_____

_____

Describe how you felt after imagining you mastered the situation.

_____

_____

_____

Plan steps to gradually de-sensitize yourself to the situation.

1. _____

2. _____

3. _____

4. _____

5. _____

Outwit Your Fears

FOR THE FACILITATOR

I. Purpose
To use humor, ridiculous exaggeration, imagery and exposure to outwit fears.

II. General Comments
Teens have fun with words and practice skills.

III. Possible Activities
a. Before the session, photocopy one *Outwit Your Fears* page; cut out the "phobia boxes" and place them near the board.
b. Photocopy one handout per participant of the remainder of the page.
c. Before the session, place a piece of paper with the word *Phobia* in large print, in the box.
d. At the start of the session, a volunteer takes the paper out of the box and shows it to the group.
e. Ask teens to raise their hands if they fear being laughed at.
f. Tell them they have *gelatophobia* (write the word on the board).
g. Ask if students know someone who has fear of teenagers (write *ephebiphobia* on the board).
h. Explain that *phobia* is an intense and irrational fear reaction.
i. Explain that volunteers take turns picking up a cutout and writing the bold text phobia on the board.
j. Peers guess the meanings and share their experiences with those fears.
k. After the ten terms have been guessed, distribute the *Outwit Your Fears* handout.
l. Emphasize the importance of defining fears in specific terms. Ex: Instead of fear of *people*, specifically state the people and the situations (e.g. decision makers at job interviews).
m. Allow time for completion.
n. Encourage teens to share their responses and receive peer feedback.

IV. Enrichment Activities
a. Read these fears and ask students to create a *phobia name* for each one.
  - Fear of failure
  - Fear of success
  - Fear of rejection
  - Fear of being different
  - Fear of a break-up
b. Encourage a discussion of these fears. Use the names given to them in section a. above.
  - Fear of failure – focus on trying your best versus meeting a specific standard.
  - Fear of success – realize you need not give in to people's demands to repeatedly out do yourself.
  - Fear of rejection – find like-minded people related to your interests, abilities, passions.
  - Fear of being different – celebrate your uniqueness.
  - Fear of a break-up – be yourself, be kind, know relationships may not survive but you will.
c. Ask for examples of how some fears *paralyze*.
  Possibilities
  - Fear failure or success – won't try.
  - Fear rejection – won't experience a loving relationship.
  - Fear being lonely – won't leave a sick relationship.
  - Fear disagreement – won't stand up for yourself or express opinions.

GOT GRIT?

Grit is perseverance (stick-to-it-tive-ness) and passion toward long term goals despite negative feedback, adversity, plateaus in progress, setbacks and failures.

Gritty people expect a marathon, not a quick win.
The tortoise had true grit; the hare had none.

Six words can tell a story.

Examples:
She practiced daily despite feeling frustrated. (had grit)

He gave up way too soon. (lost grit)

The repeated insults hurt him deeply. (needs grit)

In six words, tell how you ...

(had grit) _____

(lost grit) _____

(need grit now) _____

List ways you will develop grit.

1. _____

2. _____

3. _____

4. _____

5. _____

How *might* grit influence your outcomes?

_____

How *will* grit influence who you become?

_____

Got Grit?

FOR THE FACILITATOR

I. **Purpose**
   To define and develop grit (determination, emotional endurance).

II. **General Comments**
   Teens may be tempted to give up on their goals during difficulties.

III. **Possible Activities**
   a. Before the session, place a handful of, or a picture of gravel, coarse sand or pebbles into the box.
   b. At the start of the session, a volunteer takes the item out of the box and shows it to the group.
   c. Familiarize teens with the term *grit* (coarse granular material used in making concrete).
   d. Write this sentence on the board:
   She said 'no' the first time but he had true grit and kept asking for a date.
   e. Ask teens what "grit" means in this context (courage).
   f. Distribute the *Got Grit?* handout; a volunteer reads the explanations and examples aloud.
   g. Allow time for completion.
   h. Encourage teens to share their six word stories aloud and receive peer feedback.
   Possibilities
   The six word responses will be individualized.
   Ways to develop grit:
   - Make and work toward realistic goals.
   - Find and pursue your passion.
   - Continue trying despite set-backs and put-downs.
   - Visualize your actions toward the goal(s).
   - Work when you want to give up.
   - Make a gratitude list about your current or anticipated capabilities.
   - Accept what cannot be changed.
   - Take healthy risks to change what can be changed.
   - See positive purpose in problems.
   - Believe negative events can be manageable and meaningful.
   - Don't just do things in which you excel; try harder tasks and expect progress, not perfection.
   - Seek support from trusted family, friends and others who believe in you.
   Grit *might* influence **out**comes because you will make more progress than if you quit.
   Grit *will* influence who you **be**come – a persistent, growth-minded person.

IV. **Enrichment Activities**
   a. "Does having grit mean you will get everything you want?" (No).
   b. Write on the board: "Grit helps regulate attention, emotion and behavior in the face of temptation, distraction and difficulty."
   c. Ask teens to give examples of this type of grit.
   d. Ask teens to give examples of people they know who have grit.
   e. Ask teens to give examples of well-known people who have grit.

Self-ish-less

Self-ish = concern with own profit or pleasure; little consideration for others.
Self-less = concern with others; little consideration for one's own needs.
Self-ish-less = value own and others' needs.

In an airplane emergency, why are you told to put your oxygen mask on first before helping others?

_____

Is it self-ish? _____   Is it self-less? _____   Is it self-ish-less? _____

Balance = the Best of Both!

self-**ish**   self-**less**
_____

self-ish-less

In what situation do you struggle with selfishness and selflessness?

_____

On the above scale
Write your selfish reaction to your situation. (under "self-**ish**")
Write your selfless reaction to your situation. (under "self-**less**")
Write your balanced solution to your situation. (under "**self-ish-less**")

Example:
The Situation – A person you really like invites you to a party at 5 PM Saturday.
You promised to help at a homeless shelter at 5 PM Saturday.
    Self-ish – break your promise to the homeless shelter.
    Self-less – turn down the date.
    Self-ish-less – invite your date to help you at the homeless shelter and go to the party later.

Just for fun…create a self-ish-less tongue twister.
Example: I wish I was self-ish-less since a balance of both is best.

Self-ish-less

FOR THE FACILITATOR

I. Purpose
To cope with balancing one's own needs with consideration for others.

II. General Comments
Selfishness is usually perceived as negative; selflessness is applauded.
Teens learn that both have merits.

III. Possible Activities
  a. Before the session, place a picture of an airplane or a toy airplane into the box.
  b. Before the session, prepare a volunteer to grab the airplane from the facilitator and say "I want this!"
  c. At the start of the session, the volunteer takes the item out of the box and says "I want this!"
  d. Ask the group what behavior was portrayed (selfishness, rudeness, etc.).
  e. Pose this hypothetical situation: "A high school senior earned a scholarship to her chosen university in another state. Her family wants her to go to college close to home to work part time in the family business. Is it selfish to accept the scholarship?"
  f. Encourage discussion and debate.
  g. Ask how the person could find a balance (accept the scholarship; help family during school breaks).
  h. Distribute the *Self-ish-less* handout; a teen reads the definitions aloud.
  i. Discuss the airplane analogy (one must be alive with adequate oxygen in order to help others).
  j. Point out the scale that suggests finding a balance between one's own needs and others' needs.
  k. Review the directions under the scale with the group.
  l. Remind teens that tongue twisters are phrases, sentences or rhymes that have similar sounds.
  m. Allow time for completion.
  n. Encourage teens to share their responses and receive peer feedback and additional suggestions.
  o. Challenge teens to a contest to see how fast they can repeat each others' tongue twisters.
  p. What can a person do to help himself if he does not care about himself or others? (See *Apathy's Mask* handout, page 55.)

IV. Enrichment Activities
  a. Provide slips of paper to each teen.
     • Teens write situations on the slips of paper anonymously and place them into a container.
     • Volunteers read papers aloud and elicit peers' selfish and selfless reactions and balanced solutions.
  b. Encourage teens to share times they acted in these ways:
     • Were selfish and the outcomes.
     • Were selfless and the outcomes.
     • Achieved a balance and the outcomes.
  c. Encourage volunteers to share a *selfishless* dilemma:
     • Note the amount of time, energy, money, etc. placed on oneself and others.
     • If oneself or others absorb too much, rebalance.
  d. Elicit examples of unreasonable demands disguised as requests to be unselfish.
     Possibilities
     • To discount dreams and ambitions
     • To ignore talents
     • To compromise values
     • To risk health and safety
     • To be silent when one needs to speak
  e. Prompt teens to respond to the above demands through respectfully asserting plans to develop talents, pursue passions, stick to convictions, speak up for one's own and others' rights, etc.

Hurt Feelings – What Helps and What Hurts?

YES

Place a positive coping cutout on each (+) sign.
Write as many additional helpful hints as you can think of on the blank squares.

+						+
	+				+	
		+		+		
			+			
			+			
			+			
			+			

Hurt Feelings – What Helps and What Hurts?

NO

Place a negative reaction on each (-) sign.
Write as many additional hurtful reactions as you can think of on the blank squares.

−						−
−	−					−
−		−				−
−			−			−
−				−		−
−					−	−
−						−

Hurt Feelings – What Helps and What Hurts?

GAME INSTRUCTIONS

Cut out the boxes.
Write your own positive and negative actions in the blank squares.
Place positive actions on the YES game board.
Place negative actions on the NO game board.

Identify my inside issue that was triggered.	Give power to the person who hurt me.	"I can't control what others do."	Never trust anyone.	Get revenge.	Skip school or work due to sadness.	Feel sorry for myself.
Allow time to heal.	Judge myself and/or others.	"What did I learn?"	Bottle up my feelings.	Lash out.	"It's not normal to feel hurt."	
"I know I allow myself to have hurt feelings."	The pain is my identity.	Express my feelings.	Give up.	"There's no way out."	Choose to let go.	Relive the situation over and over.
"Who was I before this happened?"	Play the blame/ victim game.	Value everyone's opinion of me.	Forgive myself and/or others.	"Someone else hurt my feelings."	Isolate.	"I am responsible for my attitude."
			Stay trapped in the past.			

Hurt Feelings – What Helps and What Hurts?
FOR THE FACILITATOR

I. Purpose
To identify helpful and hurtful responses to hurt feelings (feeling rejected, ridiculed, put-down, etc.).

II. General Comments
Ended relationships, destructive criticism, untrue accusations, being bullied, etc., may happen.

III. Possible Activities
a. Before the session, have scissors and glue sticks or tape available.
b. Before the session, place a picture of a person who is sad or crying into the box.
c. At the start of the session, a volunteer takes the picture out of the box and shows it to the group.
d. Ask teens to brainstorm situations that could result in hurt feelings; a volunteer lists them on the board.
e. Write "Core Issue" on the board; ask its meaning (feelings within that are triggered by outside events).
f. Elicit examples: Feeling powerlessness and/or unworthy, comparing oneself with others, lack of self love, a history of being excluded, placing too much value on external circumstances, a sense of entitlement (thinking one should be spared discomforts and disappointments that are part of life experiences, etc.).
g. Distribute the three pages of *Hurt Feelings – What Helps and What Hurts?* – pages 45, 46 and 47.

Individual Format
Each teen completes the activity using the three handouts; teens compare responses and share ideas they wrote onto blank squares.
Board Activity
Copy the "YES" and "NO" game boards onto the white board, with the plus (+) and minus (-) signs. Teens take turns reading aloud the plus and minus responses and taping them to the appropriate game board.
Teens take turns writing their ideas onto the blank game boards.

YES Answer Key	NO Answer Key
+ Identify my inside issue that was triggered.	- Never trust anyone.
+ "I know I allow myself to have hurt feelings."	- Get revenge.
+ Allow time to heal.	- Play the blame/victim game.
+ "I am responsible for my attitude."	- Give up.
+ "Who was I before this happened?"	- Relive the situation over and over.
+ I can't control what others do.	- Feel sorry for myself.
+ Express my feelings.	- The pain is my identity.
+ "What did I learn?"	- Ignore my sensitive issue that showed up.
+ Choose to let go.	- Give power to the person who hurt me.
+ Forgive myself and/or others.	- "Someone else hurt my feelings."
	- "There's no way out."
	- Skip school or work due to sadness.
	- Stay trapped in the past.
	- It's not normal to feel hurt.
	- Judge myself and others.
	- Value everyone's opinions of me.
	- Lash out.
	- Isolate.
	- Bottle up my feelings.

IV. Enrichment Activities
Encourage teens to brainstorm ways to avoid pushing people's sensitive buttons.

Improv - Are You Tempted?

Improvisational theater lets you and your cast members create and collaborate on a story, dialogue, action and characters *in the moment* as you perform.
No scripts – just ad lib!

People in this scenario:

1. **Actors** who try to lure and tempt the central character to act in ways that could be harmful.
2. **Central character actor** who tries to resist being tempted.
3. **Actors, friends** of the central character, who try to help.
4. **Audience members** who are available to answer the central characters' questions.

Actors and audience, consider these techniques:

Tell people how you feel when pressured.

Be like an instant re-play and continue repeating the same phrase.

"Just say No."

Use the buddy system; take along a like-minded friend.

Find alternatives (other people, places and entertainment).

Talk about the consequences of giving in.

Talk about the rewards of sticking to your beliefs.

HALT — Don't get too hungry, angry, lonely or tired (these lower your resistance).

Don't hang around people who disrespect your decisions.

Know your own susceptibilities and avoid situations that entice you.

Add your own ideas:

_____

_____

_____

_____

Improv - Are You Tempted?

FOR THE FACILITATOR

I. Purpose
To tackle temptations that many teens face.

II. General Comments
Teens consider challenges to their well-being and ways to resist negative peer pressure.

III. Possible Activities
a. Before the session, place a picture of a well-known comedian into the box.
b. At the start of the session, a volunteer takes the picture out of the box and shows it to the group.
c. Write Improv on the board and elicit teens' experiences with improvisational comedy or theater.
d. Explain that teens will be players and/or active audience participants in scenarios involving temptations.
e. Ask about activities that may appear attractive but could cause harm.

Possibilities
- Bullying
- Cheating
- Drinking alcohol
- Dropping out of school
- Gossiping
- Lying
- Reacting with aggression or revenge when wronged
- Saying things on social media one would never say in person
- Shoplifting
- Sneaking out
- Stealing
- Taking drugs
- Torturing self to achieve the "perfect" body (binge/purge, excessive exercise, laxatives, starvation)
- Unsafe or unwanted sex

f. Elicit ways to resist temptation (possibilities are on the handout that teens have not yet received).
g. Distribute the *Are You Tempted? Improv* handout; volunteers read the page aloud.
h. Allow time for teens to add their own ways to handle situations and to share ideas with peers.
i. Direct volunteers to form small theatrical groups and briefly confer about the process:
   - Each cast member first decides on a particular storyline (temptation to bully, gossip, take drugs, etc.).
   - Ensure that different topics are selected by different casts to avoid repetition.
   - Actors will try to tempt the central character.
   - The central character will try to resist (using techniques from the handout and/or methods).
   - The central character may ask audience for suggestions or recruit someone to assist, e.g. a buddy.
j. Each cast of players performs for no more than five minutes.
k. After each performance, the audience claps, and the next cast performs.
l. When all have presented their plays, debrief about the techniques used to entice and resist.
m. Encourage teens to identify the skills they plan to use in anticipated real life situations.

IV. Enrichment Activities
a. Encourage a discussion about times teens gave into or resisted temptations and the outcomes.
b. Ask teens how they can avoid tempting others to act against their values (respect the word "No").
c. Suggest that teens create skits around other themes (responsibility, compassion, inclusion, etc.).

Self-Talk Tech – Delete and Replace

When you delete and replace on your computer, you change the text.
Example: "I'm not good at talking to people"
could be deleted and replaced with "I can listen to be people and be interested".

Write three negative self-talk texts; cross them out and write your replacements.

My Mental Computer Screen

49

Self-Talk Tech – Voiceover

A *voiceover* is words spoken in a movie or TV program by a person who is not seen.

Create a movie scene below with you as the leading actor experiencing a self-defeating thought.

Respond to a voiceover actor's suggestions

"Focus on what you can control, not the outcome."

_____

"Point out the possibilities in your situation."

_____

"Identify your strengths."

_____

Self-Talk Tech – Dormitory of Distress

Complete each resident's stress-producing sentence.

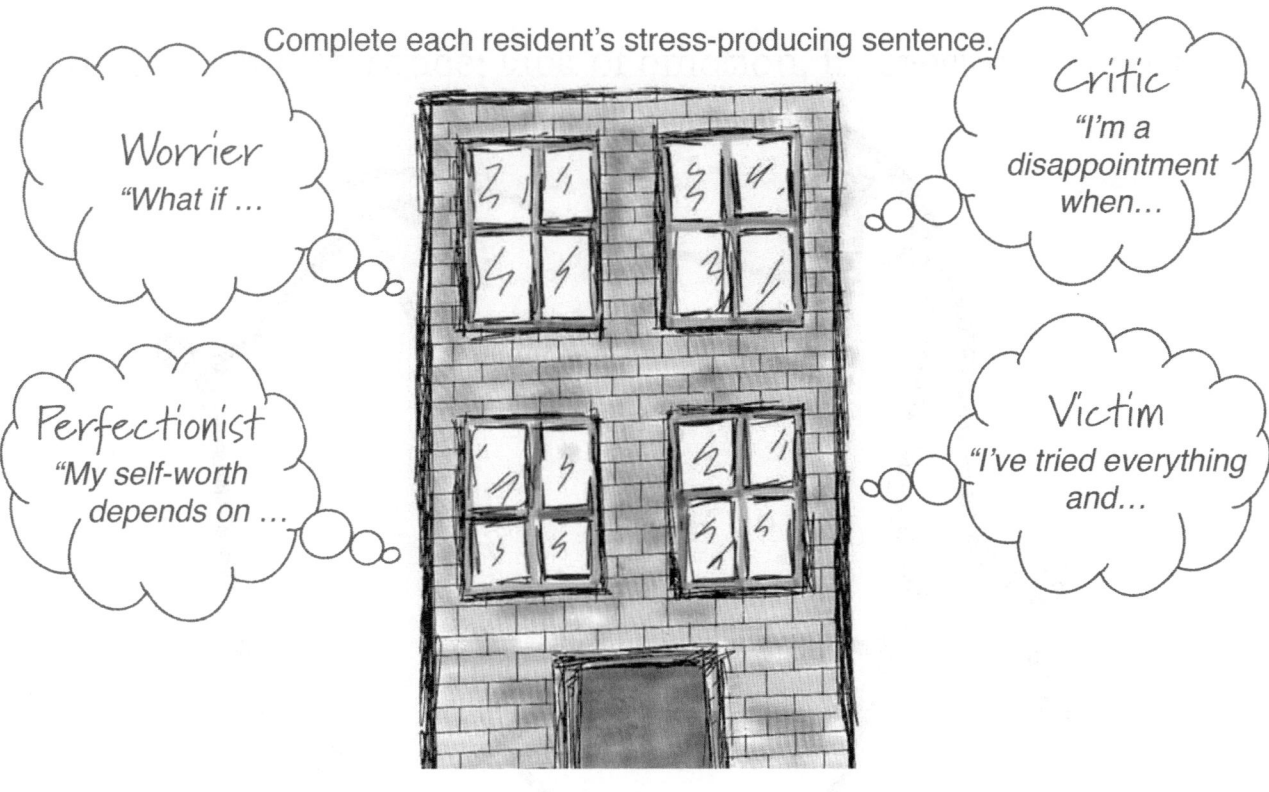

Text thought-changing ideas to each resident.
Example: Text to Worrier
Decide how to handle the worst case scenario.

Text to *Worrier*

Text to *Critic*

Text to *Perfectionist*

Text to *Victim*

Self-Talk Tech

FOR THE FACILITATOR

I. Purpose
To refute irrational ideas; to change self-defeating thoughts to positive but realistic replacements.

II. General Comments
Technology analogies help teens relate to cognitive concepts.

III. Possible Activities
a. Plan to present the *Self-Talk Tech* handouts in three consecutive sessions as a workshop or series.
b. Ideally have highlighter markers and bold point pens available.
c. Before the first session, place a cell phone or a picture of a cell phone into the box.
d. At the start of the session, a volunteer takes the item out of the box and shows it to the group.
e. Ask about its purpose (communication).
f. Ask teens ways to technologically change a letter or word (hit a CRL or other button, backspace, etc.).
g. Explain that teens will practice changing mental texts they unknowingly send to themselves.
h. Write "I'll never make the team" on the board.
i. Ask teens how the statement would affect feelings (hopeless, defeated).
j. Elicit the probable reaction (perform poorly in try-outs or not try at all).
k. Encourage teens to brainstorm positive but realistic replacement thoughts.
l. Remind teens to focus on their performance (controllable), not the outcome (beyond their control).
m. Example: "I'll try my best" rather than "I'll make the team."
n. For each *Self-Talk Tech* handout – *Delete and Replace, Voiceover,* and *Dormitory of Distress:*
   - Distribute the handout; a volunteer reads explanations and directions aloud.
   - Allow time for completion; encourage teens to share their responses and receive peer feedback.

Possible responses
   - **Delete and Replace** – texts and replacements will be individualized.
   - **Voiceover** – responses will be individualized.
   - **Dormitory of Distress** – Worrier "What if …no one wants to go out with me." Critic "I'm a disappointment … because my grades don't measure up." Perfectionist "My self worth depends on external events (winning a competition, number of friends, etc.)." Victim "I've tried everything and … nothing works for me."
   - **Examples of Texts:**
     To Worrier: "Decide how to handle the worst case scenario. To Critic: "Accept yourself"; To Perfectionist: "Expect progress not perfection;" To Victim: "Adopt an over-comer mindset".

IV. Enrichment Activities
a. Volunteers take turns writing negative sentences on the board.
b. Prompt teens to refute each thought through any or all of the following:
   - Weigh the pros and cons of holding onto the negative thought.
   - Let go of past perceived failures; identify what was learned.
   - Realize no one is perfect; identify daily improvements in your attitudes and actions.
   - Say encouraging words to yourself as you would to a friend.
   - Avoid "should", "must" or "have to."
   - Don't jump to negative conclusions; look at a situation from a possibility point of view.
   - Remember that you cannot read people's minds or predict the future.
   - Perform a reality check; ask a trusted person how the situation looks.
   - Instead of "terrific" or "terrible" know that most situations have positive and negative aspects.
   - Avoid labeling or blaming yourself or others; do not take everything personally.
   - If you are responsible for a wrongdoing, in what ways can you rectify it and/or improve?

APATHY'S MASKS

Apathy = indifference; lack of emotion, interest or concern.

Draw the face of apathy.

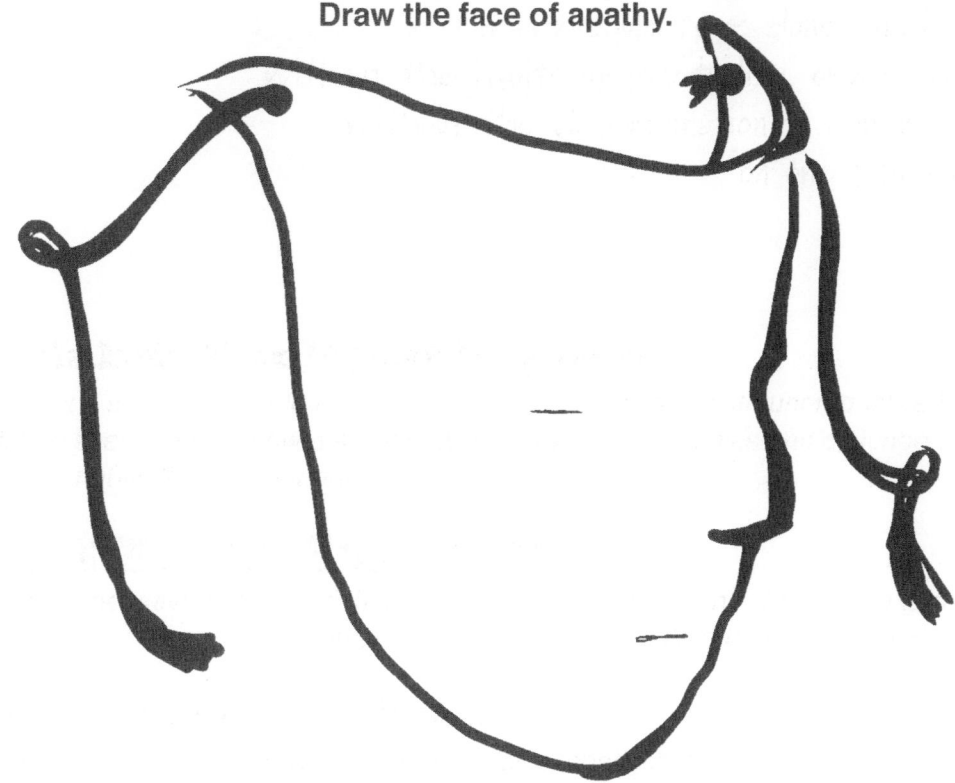

Did you ever hide behind the mask of apathy? What were the circumstances?

_____

_____

_____

_____

Place the number(s) of the cover-ups that apply to you on the face above.

1. "I don't care what you think." may mean "I do care."
2. "I'm bored" may mean "I'm lonely, empty, disconnected."
3. "What matters to you doesn't matter to me" may mean "I want to be more independent."
4. "I'll never care again" may mean "I won't risk getting hurt again."
5. "What happens to those people doesn't concern me" may mean "Only my friends matter."
6. "Life's worthless" may mean "I'm disappointed because things don't go my way."
7. "This puts me in a mellow mood" may mean "This substance helps me numb and forget my pain."
8. "Nothing matters" may mean "I'm depressed, don't enjoy life, and don't care if I live or die."

On the back of this page, draw a face that shows your REAL feelings.
You may include words, phrases, sayings and symbols.

APATHY'S MASKS

FOR THE FACILITATOR

I. Purpose
To acknowledge that apathy usually covers-up feelings that need to be recognized.

II. General Comments
"I couldn't care less" may seem cool to some, but to not care about self or others can be dangerous.

III. Possible Activities
a. Before the session, place a mask or picture of a mask into the box.
b. Before the session, ask two volunteers to practice a short mock video.
   One says, "My dog just died."
   The other shrugs shoulders and says "Whatever," and walks away.
c. At the start of the session, a volunteer takes the item out of the box and shows it to the group
d. Ask the group about the purpose of masks (to disguise or to hide).
e. Then the two actors perform; the audience claps and the volunteers return to their seats.
f. Ask the viewers what was portrayed (indifference, insensitivity).
g. Ask what could be going on with the actor who seemed uncaring (feels sorry for the person who lost the dog but does not know how to show it, or sees sharing sadness as weakness, or suffers from their own unresolved grief and loss, etc.).
h. Distribute the *Apathy's Masks* handout; a volunteer reads the definition and directions aloud.
i. Explain that for the face on the back of the page teens may show how they really feel now if they are faking apathy, or how they felt in the past when they pretended to not care.
j. Allow time for completion.
k. The face of apathy – expressionless, a phony smile, bored or tired looking, etc.
l. Encourage teens to share the numbered statements that apply to them and why.
m. Ask volunteers to elaborate about their faces and feelings drawn on the backs of their papers.
n. Ask about the advantages of sharing genuine feelings (catharsis or the relief of getting it off one's chest; others who feel the same way will know they are not alone and may open up, etc.)
o. Invite teens who have experienced apathy to share what led to and alleviated the cover-up, boredom, defiance, defensiveness, indifference, cynicism, substance abuse, and/or feelings of depression.
p. Emphasize that substance abuse, prolonged severe sadness and other serious conditions need to be shared with a trusted adult and/or acknowledged to a medical or academic professional.

IV. Enrichment Activities
Ask teens to brainstorm the dangers of apathy; a peer lists their ideas on the board.
   Possibilities
   • People who are bored may escape the emptiness by impulsive risk-taking.
   • People who act indifferent may cause others to feel excluded or emotionally abandoned.
   • People who are under the influence of substances may not consider or care about consequences.
   • People who ignore feeling depressed may harm themselves and/or others.
   • People who try to protect themselves from feeling pain eventually may not be open to experience joy.

DEVELOP HEALTHY HABITS

*I never could have done what I have done
without the habits of punctuality, order and diligence,
without the determination to concentrate myself
on one subject at a time.*

~ Charles Dickens

Chapter 3 – Develop Healthy Habits Behavioral Coping Skills

Throughout the chapter, teens will communicate through oral, written and creative expression and give and receive feedback.

Teens: Skills in each activity.
Facilitators: Competencies to evaluate.

New Habits Don't Just Happen
- Practice making beneficial decisions.
- Identify unhealthy habits to cast off.
- State positive habits to take on.
- Describe consequences of unhealthy habits that motivate change.
- Substitute a positive gain for every negative habit to give up.

It's the "Habits Game Show"
- List negative habits people may have.
- Describe a positive alternative action for each negative habit identified.
- Give examples of positive traits to adopt.

Launch and Lift Your Habits
- Name a new positive habit to plan to demonstrate.
- List reminders that motivate.
- State actions to practice the new habit.
- Identify rewards that will result.
- Describe habits of most successful people.

The Milestone Moment
- Plot a path to a healthy habit goal.
- State a simple first step.
- Explain a plan to gradually increase efforts.
- Describe the point on the path where one knows one will not turn back.
- Identify unnecessary steps that can be eliminated.

New Habits Don't Just Happen

Serpents grow and transform as they shed old skin.
See yourself as a wise serpent and draw it in the box below.
Create your serpent with scales and label the scales to show habits you want to cast off.

Serpents crawl out of their old skin to reveal a new, larger, brighter layer underneath.
Create another serpent and label the new scales to show habits you want to take on.

New Habits Don't Just Happen

FOR THE FACILITATOR

I. Purpose
To extinguish destructive habits and establish constructive habits.

II. General Comments
Teens are encouraged to let go of unproductive habits and adopt positive ones.

III. Possible Activities
a. Before the session, place a toy serpent or a picture of a serpent into the box.
b. At the start of the session, a volunteer takes the item out of the box and shows it to the group.
c. Ask teens what a serpent signifies to them (teens may note evil connotations of serpents but point out that they demonstrate transformation).
d. Distribute the *New Habits Don't Just Happen* handout.
e. A volunteer reads the text and directions aloud.
f. Instruct teens to use drawings, symbols and/or words to show their old and new scales.
g. Allow time for completion.
h. Encourage teens to share their responses and receive peer feedback.

IV. Enrichment Activity
a. Ask for a volunteer to remove a sock pulling it off from the top cuff.
b. Explain that serpents remove their skins.
c. Ask "If serpents have no hands, how do they pull off their skins?"
Elicit that they rub against rocks or rough surfaces to peel off their skins.
d. Ask teens to identify *rough spots* they encounter that prompt them to shed old habits.
   Possibilities
   • Consequences of using alcohol and drugs
   • Low grades due to poor study habits
   • Misery because of an unhealthy romance
e. Encourage teens to substitute a positive gain for every negative habit they give up.
   Possibilities
   • Give up substance abuse, gain health and clear-headedness
   • Give up disorganization, gain self-discipline and better grades
   • Give up an unhealthy romance, learn what traits do and don't work in relationships

IT'S THE "HABITS GAME SHOW"

Below list ten negative habits people may have and one positive substitution for each.
When you give clues, you will lead your partner with one word hints about the substitution.

Example: If the habit is junk food, the substitution could be vegetables.
Your one word hints could be "carrots," "crunchy," "vitamins," etc.

Negative Habits	Positive Alternative Actions
1.	1.
2.	2.
3.	3.
4.	4.
5.	5.
6.	6.
7.	7.
8.	8.
9.	9.
10.	10.

IT'S THE "HABITS GAME SHOW"

FOR THE FACILITATOR

I. Purpose
To substitute productive alternative actions for unhealthy habits.

II. General Comments
Teens may procrastinate, quit easily, cheat, lie, spend too freely, act impulsively, engage in compulsive behaviors, e.g., drinking, drugging, gambling, self-harming, playing video games excessively, etc.

III. Possible Activities
a. Before the session, place junk food or a cigarette, or a picture of either, in the box.
b. At the start of the session, a volunteer takes the item out of the box and shows it to the group.
c. Ask what the item represents (an unhealthy food, drink or substance).
d. Encourage a discussion of habits teens may wish to adopt (better study habits, healthy eating, a clean and sober lifestyle, safe self-expression, assertiveness, kindness; and motivation to save money, plan ahead, stick to a schedule, etc.)
e. Explain that teens will play a simulated game show with one word clues.
f. Distribute the *It's the "Habits Game Show"* handout.
g. Direct teens to complete their lists.
h. Pairs of volunteers take turns at the front of the room.
i. Each partner reveals one detrimental habit and gives (up to five) one word clues for the alternative action. The other partner tries to guess.
j. Then they switch roles and the guesser becomes the clue-giver.
k. Another pair of teens takes the next turn, etc.

IV. Enrichment Activities
a. Write "molt" on the board and ask its meaning (to shed an outer covering).
b. Explain that many animal species lose a covering and replace it with new growth.
c. Suggest that teens create a poster showing the beautiful plumage (pattern, colors and arrangement of feathers) of a bird they have seen or that they imagine.
d. Direct teens to label the feathers with personality or character traits they find attractive.
e. Encourage teens to display their posters on bulletin boards for students from other classes to enjoy.

Launch and Lift Your Habits

**When air is let out of a balloon the air goes
one way and the balloon goes another way.
A rocket is launched! Exhaust comes out of the
engine nozzle at high speeds pushing it forward!**

You are part of the *Lift off Committee* for a new positive habit.

Name your rocket (habit).

_____

**Rockets require lots of fuel to overcome gravity.
Habits require *Three R's* to launch them and keep them in orbit.
Reminders, Repetition and Rewards**

Reminders

List reminders that will motivate the habit.
Example: if the habit is exercise, a reminder is "I'll be a healthier person."

1.

2.

3.

4.

5.

Repetition

Plan to practice the new habit regularly:

When? _____

Where? _____

In What Ways? _____

Rewards

Rewards that will evolve from adopting the new habit:

Rewards I can give myself:

Launch and Lift Your Habits

FOR THE FACILITATOR

I. **Purpose**
    To fuel healthy habits with reminders, repetition and rewards.

II. **General Comments**
    Teens learn to reinforce positive behaviors.

III. **Possible Activities**
    a. Before the session, place an inflated balloon or picture of a rocket into a box.
    b. At the start of the session, a volunteer takes the item out of the box and shows it to the group.
    c. The volunteer lets air out of the balloon or picks up the picture from the box.
    d. Ask what it takes to launch a balloon (air) or a rocket (exhaust from fuel).
    e. Distribute the *Launch and Lift Your Habits* handout.
    f. A volunteer reads the text and directions aloud.
        Committee Format
        *   Divide teens into "committees" they elect a secretary who will write as they brainstorm responses.
        *   Each committee decides on a habit to launch, reminders, repetition and rewards.
        *   Allow time for completion.
        *   The group re-convenes and secretaries share their teams' ideas and receive peer feedback.
        Individual Format
        *   Allow time for individuals to complete the handout.
        *   Encourage teens to share their responses and receive peer feedback.

IV. **Enrichment Activities**
    a. Write this quotation on the board
        Successful people are simply those with successful habits. ~ Brian Tracy
    b. Ask teens to brainstorm successful habits; a volunteer lists them on the board.
        Possibilities
        *   Take time to think; do not censor creative ideas.
        *   See situations from all angles.
        *   Think "possibilities" not "problems."
        *   Keep your eye on the prize; say "No" to distractions.
        *   Develop a daily plan but expect the unexpected!
        *   Welcome constructive criticism.
        *   Take healthy risks.
        *   Learn from mistakes – your own and others' mistakes.
        *   Gather the info; then trust your instincts.
        *   Improve your strengths rather than worrying about weaknesses.
        *   Choose positive friends and role models.
        *   Do what's in front of you; stick with your work.
        *   Know what you will and will not sacrifice to meet your goal.

© 2013 WHOLE PERSON ASSOCIATES, 101 W. 2ND ST., SUITE 203, DULUTH MN 55802 • 800-247-6789

The Milestone Moment

Draw a squiggle (a twisted or wiggly line) to show your path to a new habit.

Draw or describe your path:

Desired habit at your squiggle's end point.

Simple start where your squiggle begins.

Steps to gradually increase your efforts along your path.

Make a marker on the Milestone Moment when you are inspired to keep going and know you will not turn back.

The Milestone Moment

FOR THE FACILITATOR

I. Purpose

To find the point in habit formation where one is compelled to reach one's goal.

II. General Comments

To take an easy first step and identify the milestone moment to develop new behaviors.

III. Possible Activities

   a. Before the session, place a sign with large letters that says, KEEP ON GOING!

   b. At the start of the session, a volunteer takes the sign out of the box and shows it to the group.

   c. Encourage teens to share positive habits they would like to develop and why.

   d. Promote a discussion about ways to develop these positive habits.

     Possibilities

- Desired habit – Walk thirty minutes daily.
- Simple start – Walk five minutes today.
- Steps to gradually increase efforts – Add five minutes every two days.
- The Milestone Moment – The twenty minute mark; now thirty minutes seems easily do-able.

   e. Distribute *The Milestone Moment* handout; a volunteer reads the directions aloud.

   f. Allow time for completion.

   g. Encourage teens to share their responses and receive peer feedback.

   h. Ask about the value of recognizing one's milestone moment (it becomes a landmark of progress; can be rewarded as a short-term goal; it makes the full-fledged habit more easily attainable, etc.).

IV. Enrichment Activities

   a. Ask teens what it means to streamline a task (make it more simple).

   b. Elicit ways to eliminate unnecessary steps when developing a habit.

     Possibilities

Habit	Streamline
Exercise thirty minutes daily.	Exercise at home instead of the gym.
Study two hours daily.	Make study space at home versus going to the library.
Drive a friend who uses a wheelchair to games.	Keep junk out of the trunk to fit the wheelchair easily.

MANAGE SOCIAL MEDIA

Honesty and transparency make you vulnerable.
Be honest and transparent anyway.
~ Mother Theresa

Chapter 4 – Manage Social Media Behavioral Coping Skills

Throughout the chapter, teens will communicate through oral, written and creative expression and give and receive feedback.

Teens: Skills in each activity.
Facilitators: Competencies to evaluate.

Social Media Roving Reporter
- Describe how most people present themselves online.
- State what could be happening behind a picture or portrayal of perfection.
- Identify ways to combat social media envy.
- Give examples of ways people cry out for help online.
- Describe ways to respond if aware of cries for help.

Find the Hidden Picture
- Illustrate one's own potentially negative aspect.
- Demonstrate a decision – to share or not to share this information in the group.
- State situations in which it is helpful to share innermost issues.
- Identify situations in which it is not safe to reveal personal information.

My Reality Site
- Create a simulated online profile that reveals authentic qualities.
- Describe pictures that show one not looking the best.
- State what matters most that others may not think is cool.
- Identify aspects of this profile to post or not post online.
- State the differences between friends who are only online and in-person friends.
- Describe the effects of social networking on emotional intimacy.

The Power of an Icon
- Demonstrate ways to be a positive role model.
- Create a positive media message about a potentially controversial issue.
- Identify one's personal media method.
- Convey ideas via a performance or a written or illustrated communication.
- Create messages to replace potentially harmful magazine or other ads, photos or articles.

Social Media Roving Reporter

I. **A roving reporter writes "Say It in One Word" on the board and asks the audience for one word responses.**

    1. The way we often present ourselves on social media is …

    2. How we might feel compared to others' online images is …

II. **A roving reporter writes "Behind This Scene" on the board and asks volunteers for the following:**

    1. Draw the "perfect family" in the board. What do you see?
       What else could be going on behind this scene?

    2. Draw the "perfect couple" on the board. What do you see?
       What else could be going on behind this scene?

    3. Ask volunteers to draw other "perfect pictures" and ask "behind this scene" questions.

III. **A roving reporter writes "On Second Thought" on the board and provides these prompts:**

    1. You see someone with a zillion "likes" and tons of friends.
       On second thought, what types of "friends" might some of them be?

    2. You see a winner of many awards.
       On second thought, what went into winning?

    3. Ask volunteers to share other profiles and ask "on second thought" questions.

IV. **A roving reporter writes "A Tiny Piece" on the board and provides these prompts …**

    1. A person shows lots of party pictures and posts about all the fun.
       If parties are a tiny piece of the person's life, what might some real life segments look like?

    2. A person shares lots of expensive events and purchases.
       If excessive spending is a tiny piece of life, what might this person need that money cannot buy?

    3. Ask volunteers to give other examples of exciting posts and ask "a tiny piece" questions.

V. **A roving reporter concludes the program by asking the audience this question:**

When we see online images, how does it help to ask ourselves "What's beyond the first impression?"

Social Media Roving Reporter

FOR THE FACILITATOR

I. **Purpose**
   To reduce the tendency to compare oneself to peers' glamorized personas.

II. **General Comments**
   Teens are encouraged to think about the realities behind contrived online facades.

III. **Possible Activities**
   a. Before the first session, place a picture of a seemingly happy family or a group of people at a party into the box.
   b. At the start of the session, a volunteer takes the picture out of the box and shows it to the group.
   c. Ask teens how they feel when they see peers' posts about wonderful aspects of their lives. (Accept any responses).
   d. Write "Social Media Envy" on the board; ask its meaning (discontent with one's own life in comparison to someone else's perceived perfection, popularity, success, etc.).
   e. Explain that teens will volunteer to be roving reporters and audience participants.
   f. Use one master copy of the *Social Media Roving Reporter* handout.
   g. Roving reporters take turns following the handout's directions.
   The first one conducts the "Say It in One Word" segment, the second does "Behind This Scene" etc.
   Possible responses
      i. "Say It in One Word"
        1. Cool, popular, funny, etc.
        2. Inadequate, unattractive, boring
      ii. "Behind this Scene"
        1. "Perfect family" – you see smiles and hugs; behind this scene may be addiction, conflict, etc.
        2. "Perfect couple" – you see a glow; behind this scene may be jealousy, a future break up, etc.
        3. Responses based on audience pictures.
      iii. "On Second Thought"
        1. "Likes" and "friends" – you see popularity; some "friends" may be mere acquaintances.
        2. Awards – what went into winning may have been much time, energy, effort, sacrifice, etc.
        3. Responses based on volunteers' profiles and questions.
      iv. "A Tiny Piece"
        1. Partygoer – some real life segments could be eating, sleeping, studying, boredom, etc.
        2. Spender – what money cannot buy includes love, self-esteem, generosity, compassion, etc.
        3. Responses based on volunteers' posts and questions.
      v. Why ask ourselves the question? The question helps us to look beyond the face-value of images and recognize that others, like us, experience ups, downs, successes and setbacks, etc.

IV. **Enrichment Activities**
   Encourage teens to brainstorm other questions to ask themselves about social media.
   Possibilities
   • What would one's social life be like if it depended on face-to-face and voice-to-voice contact only? (Ask an older family member or older friend.)
   • What are examples of people crying out for help online? How can we respond?

Find the Hidden Picture

Create a "Hidden Picture" page for your eyes only.

Develop a scene showing your own social media profile using a drawing, collage, cartoon, caricature, etc.

Partly conceal a symbol, sketch or word that reveals a trait or fact you'd like people to accept about you but one you would not put on your social media profile.

Find the Hidden Picture

FOR THE FACILITATOR

I. Purpose
To reveal a potentially objectionable aspect about oneself through a simulated hidden picture game.

II. General Comments
Teens test the waters by making a vulnerability visible, and then decide whether and when to share.

III. Possible Activities
a. Before the session, place a hidden picture puzzle or "Where's Waldo?" print-out into the box.
b. At the start of the session, a volunteer takes the item out of the box and shows it to the group.
c. Remind teens of the magazine activity they may have done when younger and of online versions.
d. Encourage a discussion of the photos and activities people show online.
e. Ask about the images most want to convey (attractive, popular, traits that lead to "fitting in" etc.).
f. Discuss characteristics many would hide (anything they think they wouldn't be accepted, etc.).
g. Distribute the *Find the Hidden Picture* handout.
h. A volunteer reads the directions aloud.
i. Advise teens to omit their names on their papers.
j. Allow time for completion.
k. Explain that playing a game is optional; those who decline put away their papers and observe peers.
l. Invite volunteer players to submit their pictures for a group game:
   • Make sure no names are on the pages.
   • Shuffle the pile of pictures.
   • Players take turns picking up a picture and holding it up for peers to view.
   • Alternatively post the pictures on the wall or pass them around the room.
   • Players examine the pictures and find the hidden symbol, drawing or word in each.
   • Take the pictures off the wall and place on a table.
   • Teens discretely take back their own papers or leave them to be shredded.
   • Encourage teens to share how it felt to view their own a hidden quality.
   • Ask how it felt when others spotted the trait.

IV. Enrichment Activities
Promote a discussion of whether and when to tell people about a difference.
   Possibilities
   • In a group of acquaintances, one might not reveal innermost fears.
   • Among true friends who respect their convictions, one could share spiritual beliefs.
   • With a trusted counselor, one would reveal a troublesome secret.

My Reality Site

Imagine a social media site with a "reality" theme.

Create your profile using your own ideas and/or some of these…
Anything and Everything that Makes Me … "Me"
"Selfies" Never Seen Before
My Actual Bio
My Inside Story
What Matters Most to Me

How would it feel to get lots of "likes" for your *real deal?* _____

_____

What parts of this profile do you think you may share? _____

_____

What parts would it be better not to share? _____

_____

My Reality Site

FOR THE FACILITATOR

I. Purpose

To celebrate uniqueness, imperfect images, genuine autobiographical data, inside info and passions.

II. General Comments

Teens are encouraged to show inner, authentic selfhood instead of superficial and embellished images.

III. Possible Activities

a. Before the session, place a piece of paper with the words REALITY SITE, in large print, into the box.

b. At the start of the session, a volunteer takes the item out of the box and shows it to the group.

c. Ask teens to share their favorite reality shows on television.

d. Elicit teens' opinions about "Are most people's social media profiles more like fantasy or reality?"

e. Ask teens to brainstorm what might appear on a reality-based website profile.

Possibilities
- People who don't look their best.
- Untouched-up photos.
- An argument instead of a smiling couple.
- An evening at home instead of a glamorous party.
- A concern or doubt rather than a superficial success story.
- Opinions that differ from the majority.
- One's passion for an occupation others may consider insignificant.

f. Distribute the *My Reality Site* handout.

g. A volunteer reads the directions aloud.

h. Allow time for completion.

i. Remind teens about confidentiality "What is said in this room stays in this room."

j. Encourage teens to share parts of their profiles within their comfort zones.

k. Prompt a generic discussion about the types of info teens would not want on their site.

Possibilities
- Private info about family members, friends and/or themselves.
- Info they would not want an employer or college admissions counselor to view.
- Info that could hurt someone's feelings or reputation.

IV. Enrichment Activities

Encourage discussion and debate about the following:
- What are differences between "friends" who are only online and in-person friends (who may also be online)?
- What are the similarities?
- In what ways does social networking encourage emotional intimacy?
- In what ways does it camouflage emotional intimacy?

The Power of an Icon

Think about students who are younger than you and impressionable.
Pretend you are a teen icon they look up to, an identity they may try on.
Decide on your message, media method and ideas to convey.

MESSAGE POSSIBILITIES

Appearance, body image, clothes	Parties
Cash, lavish lifestyle	Popularity
Coolness	Safety
Dating relationships	Sex
Decisions	Sports
Equality	Substances
Friendships	Ways to treat people
Fun	Other_____
Humanitarianism	Other_____

MEDIA POSSIBILITIES

Advertisement	Reality show clip
Dance routines	Song lyrics, music video
Documentary clip	Sports show replay
Internet blog, video, website	Television commercial or skit
Magazine spread	Other_____
Movie clip, sci. fi., fantasy, drama, comedy	Other_____

My message _____

_____

_____

My media _____

_____

_____

My ideas _____

_____

_____

_____

_____

_____

_____

The Power of an Icon

FOR THE FACILITATOR

I. Purpose
To recognize celebrities' influence for better or worse; to create positive media messages.

II. General Comments
As teens simulate icons for younger fans they may wisely discern the qualities of their own role models.

III. Possible Activities
a. Before the session, place magazines about teens, celebrities, fashion, sports, etc., into the box.
b. Gather large poster paper, markers, tape and scissors for advertisements, magazine spreads, etc.
c. At the start of the session, a volunteer takes the item out of the box and shows it to the group.
d. Ask teens what magazines and different types of media promote (what's "in" and what's "out", etc.).
e. Encourage a discussion about teens' favorite celebs and their looks, activities, etc.
f. Ask about icons' positive attitudes and actions (go after your dreams, start a charity, etc.).
g. Promote discussion about negative examples (drinking, disobeying the law, rudeness, etc.).
h. Distribute *The Power of an Icon* handout; a volunteer reads the directions and choices aloud.
i. Tell teens they only need to fill in the blanks at the bottom of the page, not finalize their creations yet.
j. Allow time for completion.
k. Encourage teens to share their responses and receive peer feedback.
l. Explain that teens will finish their media messages on the backs of handouts or using other supplies.
m. Emphasize that the projects are simulations based on the premise that they are celebrities.
n. Advise teens that *clips* and other presentations will be two to three minutes.
o. Comment that perfect spelling, grammar and artistic ability are not needed for this project.
p. Remind teens that their theoretical younger fans may copy the attitudes and behaviors they portray.
   Individual Format
   • Teens complete their messages independently then share their written or illustrated messages.
   • Those who choose to perform will present their clips, commercials, mock-videos, etc.
   • Peers provide feedback.
   Team Format
   • Teens who chose similar messages and media methods work together on a team project.
   • Teams share their written or illustrated messages or perform for peers and receive feedback.

IV. Enrichment Activities
a. Provide magazines for teens to examine for positive and negative media messages.
b. Direct individuals or teams to cut out ads, photos, etc., and attach them to poster paper.
c. Teens may want to compare and contrast the cutouts or create replacement messages.
   Possibilities
   • Next to a super thin model's photo, teens may draw a curvy person.
   • Next to a photo showing materialism, teens may draw a celeb raising money to fight poverty.
   • Next to a nasty blog, teens may write an article about kindness.

STAND UP FOR SELF AND OTHERS

Trust your own instincts, go inside, follow your heart.
Right from the start, go ahead and stand up for what you believe in.

~ Leslie Ann Warren

Chapter 5 – Stand Up for Self and Others Behavioral Coping Skills

Throughout the chapter, teens will communicate through oral, written and creative expression and give and receive feedback.

Teens: Skills in each activity.
Facilitators: Competencies to evaluate.

I Could Stand Up
- Describe a situation in which a person is being mistreated.
- Define non-violent ways to defend oneself.
- State non-violent ways to advocate for others.
- Identify types of people who are difficult to stand up to and why.
- Give examples of standing up for oneself.
- Share times one wishes one had stood up for others.

Cruelty and Courage Story Board
- Create a story board that illustrates a famous quotation about cruelty and/or courage.
- Compose a personal quotation about cruelty and/or courage.
- State ways in which it helps to know that cruelty springs from weakness.
- Share an example of standing up to friends.

Assertiveness Techniques
- Demonstrate assertiveness techniques.
- Identify which techniques peers have portrayed.
- Define individual rights that respect personal needs without violating others' rights.

Shake It Off
- Describe ways to bounce back from put-downs.
- Identify ways to use destructive criticism or other attacks to improve oneself or circumstances.
- Present research about people who rose above discrimination to become human rights leaders.

What's Going on Here?
- Share a personal interpretation of words written by a person who bullies.
- Identify the possible feelings and motivations of a person who mistreats others.
- State actions to take if displacing negative feelings onto others.
- Describe what to do if a peer shows signs of wanting to harm self or others.
- Demonstrate empathy.
- Demonstrate respect.
- Demonstrate a non-judgmental attitude.

I Could Stand Up

Write a situation in which a person is being mistreated.

Situation Box

Pass the paper.
Each player adds a short suggestion.

If I were being treated this way I could stand up for myself in a non-violent way …

1. _____

2. _____

3. _____

4. _____

5. _____

**If I saw someone else being treated this way I could stand up for
the person in a non-violent way …**

1. _____

2. _____

3. _____

4. _____

5. _____

I Could Stand Up

FOR THE FACILITATOR

I. **Purpose**
    To identify verbal, non-violent, ways to stand up for oneself and others.

II. **General Comments**
    Teens write scenarios about peers who bully, adults who dash their dreams, people who exclude them, etc.

III. **Possible Activities**
    a. Before the session, place a picture of a swimming pool, or people in a pool, into a box.
    b. At the start of the session, a volunteer takes the picture out of the box and shows it to the group.
    c. Ask teens to raise their hands if they have seen someone thrown into the water, or have been thrown in themselves.
    d. Encourage a discussion about how it feels to be the person who gets dunked (surprised, embarrassed).
    e. Ask what the person who didn't like being thrown in said. (Never do that again!)
    f. Ask how a bystander could help. (Say "stop" as they see the person about to do it; walk away with the person after the person got out of the pool).
    g. Distribute the *I Could Stand Up* handout, and a different colored pencil for each teen, if available; a volunteer reads the directions aloud.
    h. Encourage a brief discussion of possible situations.
        Possibilities
        *   Being bullied, put down due to a difference, laughed at, excluded
        *   Being told one's dreams are unrealistic, goals are unreachable, ability and talent are lacking
    i. Explain the game-play.
        *   Each teen writes a scenario in the Situation Box.
        *   The papers are then passed around to the next person.
        *   Each teen writes a suggestion on any blank (regarding standing up for oneself or the other person).
        *   The passing of papers continues as players add suggestions.
        *   When the papers have been passed ten times all the blanks will be filled in.
        *   Each person holding a completed paper reads the scenario and suggestions aloud.
        *   Players provide feedback about the ideas.
        Possible suggestions for defending self and others
        *   Use an "I feel …" statement; consider how the person may feel.
        *   Say "No!" Tell perpetrators "No means NO!"
        *   Say "Stop!" Tell perpetrators "Stop means STOP!"
        *   Explain "I respect your advice but …"
        *   Discuss the situation with a trusted adult.
        *   Call 911 or the local emergency services number if danger is imminent.

IV. **Enrichment Activities**
    a. Encourage teens to discuss, without naming names, people in their lives who are difficult to stand up to and why.
        Possibilities
        *   Friends because of the need to fit in
        *   Parents because of the need for their approval
        *   Bullies because they seem powerful
        *   Well-meaning advisors because they do not understand another's passion
    b. Encourage teens to elaborate about times they have stood up for themselves.
    c. Ask volunteers to share times they wish they had stood up for others.
    d. Prompt teens to identify ways to stand up for themselves in current challenges.
    e. Prompt teens to identify ways to stand up for others in current challenges.

Cruelty and Courage Storyboard

Create a storyboard (a sequence of drawings or cartoons).
Add captions and/or speech balloons.
Depict scenes on the template below or use a separate sheet of paper for each scene.
Illustrate one of the quotations below or compose your own.

All cruelty springs from weakness.

~ Lucius Annaeus Seneca

It takes a great deal of bravery to stand up to our enemies,
but just as much to stand up to our friends.

~ J. K. Rowling

Courage is what it takes to stand up and speak; courage is also
what it takes to sit down and listen.

~ Winston Churchill

My own quotation …

"_____

_____"

~ _____

AUTHOR OF QUOTATION

Cruelty and Courage Storyboard

FOR THE FACILITATOR

I. Purpose
To use visual thinking and planning to reinforce concepts about cruelty and courage.

II. General Comments
Teens create illustrations and dialogue to bring quotations to life.

III. Possible Activities
a. Before the session, place tape and several pieces of computer paper into the box.
b. At the start of the session, a volunteer picks up the papers from the box and tapes them across the board.
c. Ask teens to imagine an illustration or cartoon on each paper.
d. Explain that people can tell a story visually, as in a comic book, through a series of pictures.
e. Distribute the *Cruelty and Courage* handout; a volunteer reads the directions and quotes aloud.
f. Emphasize that artistic ability is not needed; teens may use stick figures, symbols, etc.
g. Any team or individual may write a quotation and then illustrate the message.

Team Format
- Divide teens into teams according to the quote they wish to address.
- Teammates collaborate to create several scenes with captions and/or speech balloons.
- The group re-convenes, and teams tape their papers to the board and read their dialogue aloud.
- The audience provides feedback.

Individual Format
- Individuals complete the activity using the template or several pieces of paper.
- Encourage volunteers to show their pictures and read their dialogue aloud.
- Peers provide feedback.

IV. Enrichment Activities
Pose questions related to the quotes.

Possibilities
- How does it help to know that cruelty springs from weakness?
  (People who bully may realize they show weakness, not toughness;
  those who are bullied and bystanders may be less intimidated and more assertive).
- Who is willing to describe situations in which they stood up to friends?
  (Individualized responses).
- When does it take courage to listen?
  (When hearing disappointing or sad news or constructive criticism).

Assertiveness Techniques

Fogging – agree with a truth but do not give in.
Example:

Relative:	"You shouldn't wear your hair that way; it's weird."
You:	"I know it seems extreme to you but I like it."

Instant Replay – calmly repeat the same message.
Example:

Friend:	"Please let me drive your parents' car."
You:	"Only I am allowed to drive the car."
Friend:	"They'll never know; don't be so selfish."
You:	"Only I am allowed to drive the car."

Admit and Apologize – accept accurate negative statements.
Example:

Parent/Caregiver:	"You dented the car."
You:	"Yes I did and I am so sorry."

Accept Responsibility – rectify mistakes when possible.
Example:

Parent/Caregiver:	"It's going to cost a lot to fix the dent."
You:	"I'll pay you back a little each month."

Make Needs Known – ask directly for what you want or need.
Example:

Dating Partner:	"I expect you to answer my texts immediately."
You:	"Please understand that I turn off my phone when I study."

Obtain Information – find the facts before you decide.
Example:

Friend:	"I need you to help me with my project."
You:	"What kind of help do you need?"
Friend:	"You only need to do the research and then write the paper."
You:	"I won't do the whole assignment for you."

Say "No" – and mean it.
Example:

Partner:	"Can we take our relationship to a new level?"
You:	"No!"

Assertiveness Techniques

FOR THE FACILITATOR

I. **Purpose**
   To practice assertiveness techniques.

II. **General Comments**
   Teens use the skills in skits and identify techniques that peers portray.

III. **Possible Activities**
   a. Before the session, place a picture of fog into the box.
   b. Before the session, photocopy two of the *Assertiveness Techniques* handouts and cut on the broken lines.
   c. Keep them in duplicate set stacks.
   d. At the start of the session, a volunteer takes the picture out of the box and shows it to the group.
   e. Write "Fogging" on the board and explain it is an assertiveness technique.
   f. Ask the meaning of *Assertiveness* (to stand up for personal rights – to express thoughts, feelings and beliefs in direct, honest and appropriate ways).
   g. Ask for volunteers to demonstrate techniques.
   - Give each pair of actors a different set of cutouts (two copies of the same technique).
   - The actors take turns writing their techniques with definitions on the board and demonstrating them.
   - Teens will read their lines, no need to memorize.
   h. Leave the titles on the board; collect the two cutouts from each pair and keep duplicates together.
   i. Place them in stacks of two duplicates, face-down on a table.
   j. Ask for pairs of volunteers to create different scenarios that portray techniques.
   - Pairs of actors pick up a set of two duplicate cutouts.
   - Based on the title and example, each pair writes their own script.
   - Teens write their lines on the backs of their cutouts and read aloud during their performances.
   - Encourage actors to use situations from their own lives for their skits, without naming names.
   - Advise teens that each presentation will be a couple of minutes.
   - Each actor will have one to three lines.
   - Allow a few minutes for each pair to practice.
   k. The group re-convenes.
   l. Pairs of actors present their skits.
   m. The audience claps after each performance and guesses which technique was portrayed.
   n. Ask teens which skills they plan to use in real life and in what circumstances.

IV. **Enrichment Activities**
   a. Encourage teens to brainstorm rights that respect personal needs without violating others' rights.
   b. A volunteer lists ideas on the board.
   Possibilities
       The right to …
   - Express wants and needs
   - Refuse a request without being rude or rejecting the person who asked
   - Say "No" without "I'm sorry, but…"
   - Set personal priorities
   - Establish boundaries
   - Make mistakes
   - Assert opinions
   - Decide when NOT to be assertive (choose one's battles wisely)

SHAKE IT OFF

A parable describes a donkey that fell into a pit.
He cried out for help but the farmer decided
"He's old so I'll bury him and cover the pit."
The farmer shoveled piles of dirt into the pit.
At first the donkey wailed, then became quiet.

What do you think happened?

Now here is the rest of the story…

The donkey shook off each mound of dirt and stepped up on it. When the mound was high enough; the donkey jumped out.

Imagine yourself or another person in a pit.
In a parable, picture, or both, tell …
Who is shoveling "dirt"?
What is the "dirt"?
How does the person "shake it off"?
How does the person use the "dirt" to personal advantage?

SHAKE IT OFF

FOR THE FACILITATOR

I. **Purpose**
    To prevent negativity from penetrating one's self-concept and put it to positive use.

II. **General Comments**
    Assertive behavior may not deter some cruel people; teens need internal strength and ingenuity to cope.

III. **Possible Activities**
    a. Before the session, place a picture of a donkey into the box.
    b. At the start of the session, a volunteer takes the picture out of the box and shows it to the group.
    c. Explain that teens will read a parable about a donkey.
    d. Tell teens that a parable is a single story to illustrate a moral or spiritual lesson.
    e. Distribute the *Shake It Off* handout; a volunteer reads the parable and the directions aloud.
    f. Tell teens that for this activity perfect grammar or artistic talent are not important.
    g. Allow time for completion.
    h. Encourage teens to share their parables and/or pictures and receive peer feedback.
    Possibilities
    - Who is shoveling "dirt"?
        Enemies; friends, peers who exclude or whisper or laugh; teammates, family
        People with low expectations for the person in the pit
    - What is the "dirt"?
        Destructive criticism, labels, put-downs, discrimination, bullying
    - How does the person shake it off?
        Assertive techniques (addressed in the *Assertiveness Techniques* activity, page 71.
        Positive self-talk for each put-down
        Realize that the "dirt" is the other person's own problems that are being projected onto others
        Know that cruelty springs from weakness
    - How does the person use the "dirt" to personal advantage?
        Prove the critics wrong
        Advocate for others who are bullied or beaten down
        Start a program at school to enhance empathy, curtail cruelty, stop bullying
        Become a kinder person after suffering the effects of cruelty
        Study, practice, work to do one's best while ignoring put-downs
        Remember to run one's own race without listening to comparisons
        Develop a positive support system
        Seek spiritual support to help with forgiveness.
        Create inspirational pictures, poems, songs, parables, posters, etc.
        to help other people out of pits

IV. **Enrichment Activities**
    a. Encourage teams to research people who rose above the "dirt" of discrimination to become civil rights activists, proponents for people who have differences, illnesses, disabilities, etc.
    b. Arrange for teams to present their findings in assemblies or other forums.

WHAT'S GOING ON HERE?

I'm hurting and so I lash out.
I ridicule, name-call and shout.
I need power, control and glory.
I'm *terrible* – end of story?

I fear you are out to get me
So I must top the hierarchy.
Bully and *evil* you label.
You flee from me if you're able.

To pretend to be strong is my tool,
The purpose of which is to fool
You whom I seem to hate.
I wish we could really relate.

I too have been a victim,
From this my actions stem.
I'd like to be loved and accepted.
But my behavior makes me rejected.

If I remove my tough armor
And drop my intimidating posture,
Will I be at risk of harm?
Or welcomed with open arms?

C. A. Butler

**Now, you figure out what you think is going on
with the person who wrote the poem.**

_____

_____

_____

_____

_____

_____

WHAT'S GOING ON HERE?
FOR THE FACILITATOR

I. **Purpose**
    To identify bullying as a behavior rather than label people *bullies* or *victims*.
    To understand the possible emotions and motives of teens who bully.
    To help teens who bully recognize themselves and seek help to change.

II. **General Comments**
    Many teens who bully have often been tormented or excluded at home or by peers. Some may cover feelings of inadequacy with feigned dominance and some may have an inflated self-concept.

III. **Possible Activities**
    a. Before the session, place a stick and a stone, or pictures of a stick and a stone, into a box.
    b. At the start of the session, a volunteer takes the items out of the box and shows them to the group.
    c. Ask if teens have heard the children's slogan, "Sticks and stones can break my bones but names can never hurt me."
    d. Encourage teens to discuss whether they agree or disagree with the statement and why. Elicit that spoken and written words can cause severe pain.
    e. Distribute the *What's Going on Here?* handout; volunteers read the verses and directions aloud.
    f. Allow time for completion.
    g. Ask teens which lines had the most meaning for them and why.
    h. Encourage teens to share their responses and receive peer feedback.
       Initially, accept teen responses without question to allow free expression.
       Later, some ideas may need to be re-thought.
       Responses to re-think
       The person who wrote the poem is …
         • A *bully*
         • A *victim*
         • Both *bully* and *victim*
       Teachable moment
         • Ask if the words *bully* and *victim* are identities (no) or labels (yes).
         • Ask for a more accurate description of the person. (Someone who shows bullying behavior or victim-like reactions)
       Possibilities to elicit
       What may be going on with the person who wrote the poem? The person …
         • Feels the pain of exclusion but turns it outward onto others
         • Feels inadequate but puts up a powerful front of self-confidence
         • Acts hateful and yet, really wants friends
    i. Encourage a discussion about what teens can do if they see characteristics of themselves in the poem. (Tell a trusted adult, seek counseling, etc.).
    j. Ask about ways to help people who turn inward pain outward. (If someone appears to show interest in harming self or others, tell a trusted adult; if appropriate and safe – act friendly, etc.).

IV. **Enrichment Activities**
    Encourage teens to research anti-bullying programs and approach administration with ideas to enhance existing efforts at their school or facility.

OVERCOME OBSTACLES

Obstacles are those frightful things you see when you take your eyes off your goal.
~ Henry Ford

Chapter 6 – Overcome Obstacles Behavioral Coping Skills

Throughout the chapter, teens will communicate through oral, written and creative expression and give and receive feedback.

Teens: Skills in each activity.
Facilitators: Competencies to evaluate.

MIND MAP-ABLE Solutions
- Define types of obstacles:
  Personal
  Social
  Environmental
- Identify techniques to overcome each type of obstacle.
- Create a mind map that shows a personal obstacle.
- Depict and /or describe the problem's possible opportunities.
- Show options.
- Show each option's possible outcomes.
- Debate and discuss whether or not one agrees with a quotation about being able to bear any adversity.

I Have Learned
- Describe a difficult circumstance one faced or experienced.
- Identify concepts one learned from experiencing the difficulty.
- Give an interpretation of "If life gives you lemons, make lemonade."
- Create a personal slogan for "If life gives you _____, make _____."
- Describe possible valuable outcomes of facing adversity.

Jumping Over My Hurdles
- Identify types of barriers people face.
- Draw and/or describe an emotional or situational hurdle.
- Show and/or state ways to overcome the obstacle.

Rainbow of Chaos
- Give a personal interpretation of a quotation about living in a rainbow of chaos.
- Use spirituality to depict, describe or portray the beauty seen in some types of chaos.
- Identify the personal growth experienced through facing chaos.
- Interpret analogies about the science of rainbows and facing trials.

Tapping Into My Inner Strength
- Define situations in which inner strength is needed.
- Describe ways inner strength will help solve problems.
- Respond to this sentence starter "If my inner strength were a person, what or who would be its ..."

MIND MAP-ABLE SOLUTIONS

A mind map lets you visually organize your thoughts.

Draw and/or write one of your major obstacles in the center.
Branch out from the center in many directions to show your options, possible outcomes, etc.
Your map may look like a spider (body = obstacle, legs = ideas) or
any shape that speaks to you.
Use color, symbols, words or short phrases – whatever helps you see the situation clearly.

Draw your map on the back of this page in the landscape position or in the box below.

MIND MAP-ABLE SOLUTIONS

FOR THE FACILITATOR

I. Purpose
To visualize the big picture – an obstacle with its many opportunities.

II. General Comments
A mind map with its branches or designs puts a problem and possible solutions in perspective.

III. Possible Activities
a. Before the session, place a map or a picture of a map into the box.
b. Consider having large drawing paper and color markers available.
c. At the start of the session, a volunteer takes the map out of the box and shows it to the group.
d. Ask about a map's uses (plot routes to a destination, find one's way when lost).
e. Write this Frank A. Clark quotation on the board:
   "If you find a path with no obstacles, it probably doesn't lead anywhere."
   Elicit that most people have to jump over some hurdles or find ways around them.
f. Explain that teens will create mind maps of a current challenge and its possible solutions.
g. Ask teens to give examples of obstacles people try to overcome (individualized responses).
h. Make three columns on the board "Personal Obstacles," "Social Obstacles," "Emotional Obstacles."
   Elicit examples.
   * Personal – a lack of confidence, knowledge, etc. or fears of failure, success, embarrassment, etc.
   * Social – people who are uncooperative, irresponsible, unkind, or who sabotage one's efforts, etc.
   * Environmental – stressful situations at home, school, work or a change in living conditions, etc.
i. Ask teens to brainstorm ways to overcome obstacles; a volunteer lists their ideas on the board.
   Possibilities
   * Decide what can and can't be changed, e.g., one can change one's self but not others.
   * Recall what has worked in similar situations.
   * Think about making the obstacle smaller and one's ability to conquer it greater.
j. Distribute the *MIND MAP-ABLE SOLUTIONS* handout; a volunteer reads the directions aloud. Suggest some map tips.
   * Brainstorm; experiment with new directions.
   * Show small steps toward possible outcomes.
   * Don't worry about artistic ability or spelling for this activity.
   * Plan to add ideas later when seeking suggestions from people who overcame this obstacle.
k. Allow time for completion.
l. Encourage teens to share their diagrams and receive peer suggestions that they may add to their maps.

IV. Enrichment Activities
a. Write this Marcus Aurelius quotation on the board:
   "Nothing happens to anybody which he is not fitted by nature to bear."
b. Ask teens to discuss and debate whether they agree or disagree and why.

I Have Learned ...

**Think about one of the worst circumstances you have faced or are facing
and what you have learned from this experience.**

Examples:

"I learned from being homeless that ..."
1.   I gained empathy for people with problems.
2.   I feel great when I volunteer at a shelter.

"I learned from a break up that ..."
1.   I was able to move forward.
2.   I now know what and who I am looking for in a good relationship.

The difficult situation I have faced or am facing now is _____

_____

_____

_____

I have learned ...

1. _____

_____

2. _____

_____

3. _____

_____

4. _____

_____

5. _____

_____

I Have Learned ...

FOR THE FACILITATOR

I. Purpose
To recognize that adversity can be used to strengthen character and improve quality of life.

II. General Comments
Problems that are difficult at the time promote learned coping skills, acceptance, gratitude and wisdom.

III. Possible Activities
a. Before the session, place a paper with large print titled "*Report Card*," with a big "F" on it, into the box.
b. At the start of the session, a volunteer takes the report card out of the box and shows it to the group.
c. Ask teens how they would feel if they received that grade (upset, worried).
d. Prompt teens to consider "How could a person who failed a class learn from the experience?"
   Possibilities
   • Admit the need for help.
   • Determine what their strengths are – subjects with better grades or non-academic skills.
   • Develop better study habits.
e. Encourage teens to brainstorm types of difficulties; a volunteer lists their ideas on the board.
   Possibilities
   • Addiction
   • Conflict
   • Being bullied
   • Grief and loss due to death or a relationship ending
   • Low self-esteem
   • Illness or disability
   • Poverty
f. Distribute the *I Have Learned ...* handout; a volunteer reads the directions and example aloud.
g. To safeguard anonymity, tell teens to omit their names on their papers.
h. Allow time for completion.
i. Encourage teens to share their responses and receive peer feedback.
j. Invite teens to post their pages where people from other classes or groups can add their own lists.

IV. Enrichment Activities
a. Ask teens if they have heard the saying "When life gives you lemons, make lemonade."
b. Encourage interpretation (make something positive out of what appears negative).
c. Instruct teens, as a group project, in teams or individually, to create posters.
   They will complete the sentence "If life gives you _____, make _____."
   Possibilities
   • If life gives you a difference, make a difference.
   • If life gives you a roadblock, make a new road.
   • If life gives you a limitation, make the most of your assets.

Jumping Over My Hurdles

✂

Top of the Wall Draw a ladder with rungs leaning against the wall. Write your barrier on the wall. Label the rungs to show ways to get to the top.	**Unravel It** Draw a knot. Write your difficulty under the knot. Identify the tangles and how you can loosen or cut through them.	**Possibilities** Draw a mountain. Write your obstacle on the top. Write your possible paths around, over and through it.	**Momentum** Draw a gymnastic hurdle. Write your problem on the hurdle. Show ways to get a running start to jump over it.	**Keys** Draw a door with a lock. Write what stops you on the closed door. Draw and label keys on a key ring with ways to open it. Show what's inside.
Raise the Bar Draw a high jump hurdle. Write your challenge on it. Label a few higher hurdles with ways to gradually improve your skills.	**A Reward** Draw a tunnel. Write your problem on the entrance and your reward for solving it on the exit. Note what guides you.	**Defensive Block** Draw a large football. Write what blocks you from reaching your goal under the ball. Autograph the ball with ways to reach your goal.	**Don't Put Off** Title your paper "Procrastination." Identify what you continually delay doing. Simplify what you need to do into three steps.	**Face Fright** Draw a monster. Write "Fear" on the monster and note what you fear. Label footprints with ways you'll gradually get closer to it.
Focus Write three ways you are distracted and which interfere with your progress. List ways to minimize them. Note what you plan to achieve.	**Me – A Barrier?** Draw a sad face and under it, write what you do to sabotage yourself. Draw a happy face and under it write ways to help yourself.	**Soar** Draw a crashed balloon. Write your negative thoughts about it. Draw a helium balloon with beliefs that uplift you.	**Peace Power** Title your paper "Discrimination" and note several ways people discriminate. Compose signs that promote equality.	**Get Past the Past** Write of an incident from the past that still bothers you. List positive ways to right the wrong, forgive, and help people in similar situations.

Jumping Over My Hurdles

FOR THE FACILITATOR

I. Purpose
To identify ways to cope with different types of barriers, obstacles and hurdles.

II. General Comments
Teens personalize and apply hints to help them over hurdles.

III. Possible Activities
a. Before the session:
- Place a set of keys, or a picture of keys, into a box.
- Photocopy the *Jumping Over My Hurdles* handout and cut out the fifteen squares; make additional copies and cutouts for groups larger than fifteen.
- Have paper and pens or markers available.
- Either spread the cutouts face-down on a table, to allow participants to pick their own without turning them over, or plan to distribute one cutout per person.

b. At the start of the session, a volunteer takes the keys or picture out of the box and shows it to the group.

c. Ask about a key's purpose (to unlock doors, or figure things out, e.g., the key to success and answer keys).

d. Explain that teens will focus on the keys to overcome obstacles.

e. Tell teens to pick up their own cutouts or distribute one per person.

f. Distribute paper and pens or markers.

g. Allow time for completion.

h. Encourage teens to share their responses and receive peer feedback.

IV. Enrichment Activities
a. Divide teens into teams.

b. Each team creates posters or slogans about breaking down barriers.

Possible types of barriers
- Shyness
- Disability
- Social Exclusion
- Lack of education or skills
- Abuse with seemingly no way out
- Bullying
- Low self-esteem
- Person versus person
- Person versus self
- Person versus society (political, social or economic differences)
- Group against group (cliques, cultures)

Rainbow of Chaos

We live in a rainbow of chaos.

~ Paul Cezanne

Create your rainbow of chaos.

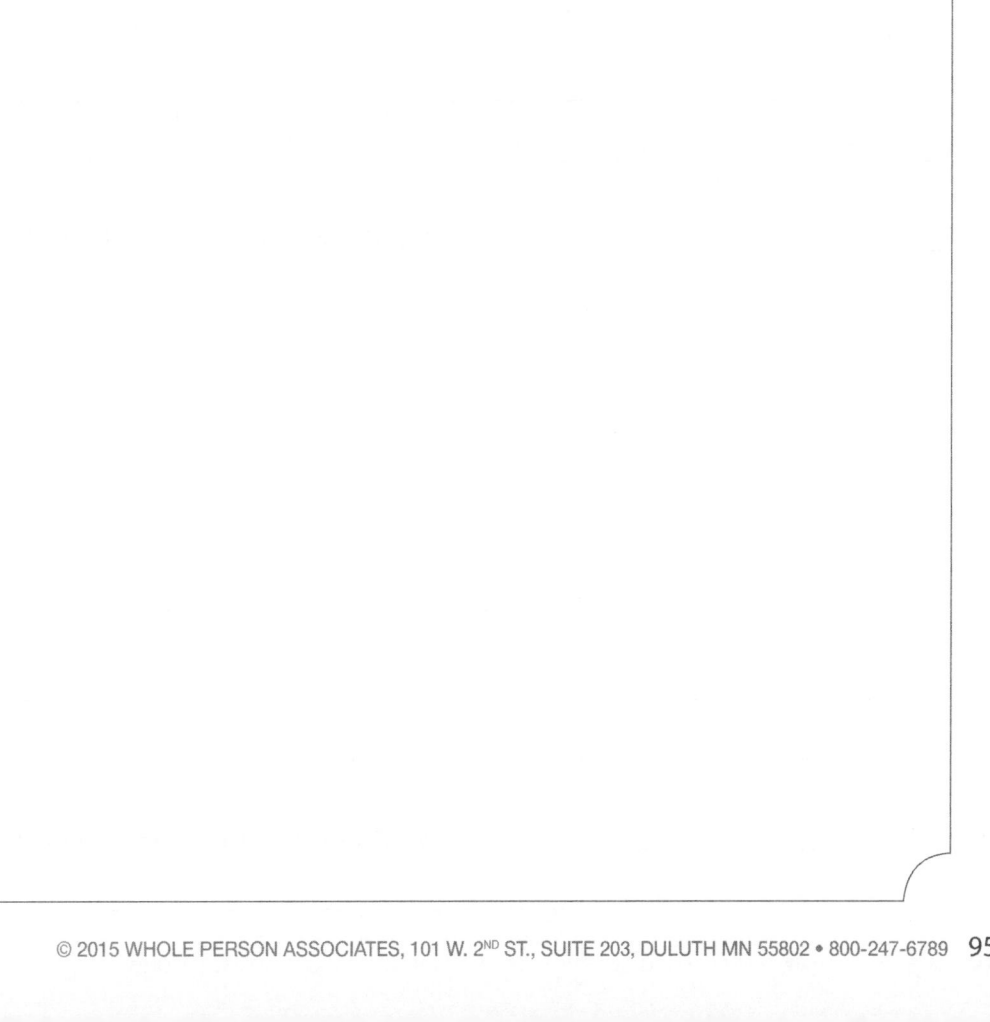

Rainbow of Chaos

FOR THE FACILITATOR

I. Purpose
To recognize that often through chaos, growth may occur.

II. General Comments
Teens apply the art and science of rainbows to life's turbulence.

III. Possible Activities
a. Before the session, place a picture of a rainbow into the box.
b. Have color markers, paints, and/or crayons available.
c. At the start of the session, a volunteer takes the picture out of the box and shows it to the group.
d. Ask teens what about rainbows comes to mind (beauty, hope, the calm after the storm, etc.).
e. Write "Chaos" on the board and ask its meaning (complete confusion and disorder).
f. Pose the question "Can there be beauty in chaos?" (yes); ask for examples.
  • A busy but productive life
  • An exciting varsity game with lots of action
  • The mess amidst a creative project
g. Distribute the *Rainbow of Chaos* handout; a volunteer reads the quote and directions aloud.
h. Explain that Cezanne was an artist and painter, however, they do not need to be artistic. They can express their scene in any way.
i. Encourage teens to use their imaginations to portray personal situations.
j. If teens need further direction copy this list onto the board:

Cartoon	Essay	Pantomime
Collage	Interpretive dance	Poem
Doodle	Lyrics	Short Story
Drawing	Maze	Squiggle

k. Examples to suggest only for teens who seem stumped:
  • Draw chaos, a dilemma or turmoil and superimpose the colors of the rainbow across the page.
  • Draw and color a rainbow and label each color with a current challenge or aspects of one challenge.
  • Describe each color's meaning in terms of the circumstance, e.g. green may signify new beginnings, orange may be the fire within that will not give up, etc.
l. Allow time for completion.
m. Encourage teens to share their responses and receive peer feedback.
  • Teens display and elaborate about their art or read their written work aloud.
  • Teens perform brief songs, dances or pantomimes.

IV. Enrichment Activities
Discuss the science of rainbows in terms of facing trials.
Examples
  • Both rain and sun (bleakness and brightness) are required.
  • People need to look for the rainbow (see the possibilities in a situation).
  • Light waves refract or bend as they enter raindrops to create color; people bend (change the direction of thoughts and actions) to bring order to chaos or to see its beauty.
  • The rainbow's colors are reflected (people reveal their true colors in how they handle both hardships and triumphs).

Tapping into My Inner Strength

INNER STRENGTH ≡ POWER, FORCE, MENTAL MUSCLE = HELPS OVERCOME OBSTACLES

Example: I need my inner strength *when I am being pressured to go out on a school night.*
I will tap into my inner strength to solve this problem by *saying I'll do homework first and if I get done in time, I'll join you.*

I need my inner strength _____

_____

I will tap into my inner strength to solve this problem by _____

_____

I need my inner strength _____

_____

I will tap into my inner strength to solve this problem by _____

_____

I need my inner strength _____

_____

I will tap into my inner strength to solve this problem by _____

_____

I need my inner strength _____

_____

I will tap into my inner strength to solve this problem by _____

_____

I need my inner strength _____

_____

I will tap into my inner strength to solve this problem by _____

_____

Tapping into My Inner Strength
FOR THE FACILITATOR

I. **Purpose**
To recognize and tap into one's inner strength.

II. **General Comments**
Inner strength helps teens overcome obstacles and reject risky reactions.

III. **Possible Activities**
a. Before the session, place an action figure toy or a picture of an action figure into the box.
b. At the start of the session, a volunteer takes the action figure out of the box and shows it to the group.
c. Ask teens what comes to mind when they see powerful figures (strength).
d. Ask teens to identify types of strength (physical, emotional, strength of character).
e. Distribute the *Tapping into My Inner Strength* handout; a teen reads the definition of inner strength, and the example, aloud.
f. Emphasize that inner strength means being strong and having the conviction to make wise choices.
   It does not mean teens are invincible regarding unsafe or unwise behavior.
g. Allow time for completion.
h. Encourage teens to share their responses and receive peer feedback.
i. Remind teens if their responses are personal, use name codes.
j. Tell them, "What is said in this room stays in this room."
   Possibilities
   I need my inner strength when… and I will tap into my inner strength to solve this problem by…
   - Someone says "No" to going out with me. *Know someone else will say "Yes."*
   - A relationship breaks up. *Believe I will have other good relationships.*
   - I'm tempted to use drugs or alcohol. *Say "No" and avoid situations where they're available.*
   - My friends pressure me to do something wrong. *Reach out to people who share my values.*
   - People at home are abusive. *Tell a trusted adult.*
   - I am being bullied. *Tell a trusted adult.*
   - I feel put down or left out. *Go places with like-minded friends.*
   - Someone says I'll never achieve my goals. *Believe I can.*
   - I receive a low grade on a test. *Ask for help.*
   - I am not accepted at my desired job or college. *Continue to pursue other jobs and schools.*
   - I make a mistake. *Admit my error and apologize.*
   - I hear constructive criticism. *Evaluate its validity, and if true, make changes.*

IV. **Enrichment Activities**
Ask teens to brainstorm responses to "If my inner strength were a person, what or who would be its …"
   - Favorite song?
   - Most frequently spoken word?
   - Slogan?
   - Most difficult challenge?
   - Proudest moment?
   - Hero?
   - Role Model?

ADVANCE BEYOND COPING = THRIVE

I've come to believe that each of us has a personal calling that's as unique as a fingerprint —
and that the best way to succeed is to discover what you love and then find a way to offer it to others in the form of service, working hard, and also allowing the energy of the universe to lead you.

~ Oprah Winfrey

Chapter 7 – Advance Beyond Coping – Thrive Behavioral Coping Skills

Throughout the chapter, teens will communicate through oral, written and creative expression and give and receive feedback.

Teens: Skills in each activity.
Facilitators: Competencies to evaluate.

In the Future, My World
- Read a poem about the Earth and note the different meanings when read forward and backward.
- Identify a humanitarian or other issue that needs attention.
- Write a personal poem.
- Define ways to use various abilities to promote awareness of an issue.
- Debate the pros and cons of peaceful demonstrations.
- Identify other ways a message can be conveyed.
- State some ways to raise funds.
- Identify the benefits received from volunteering.
- Share a plan to follow through on advocacy or humanitarian efforts.

My Pearls Within
- Describe one's own inner wisdom or positive qualities.
- State plans to cultivate inner wisdom or positive qualities with enthusiasm.
- Describe an action one is determined to take.
- State ways a problem can bring out one's best qualities as an irritant helps create a pearl.

Night Sky Inspirations
- Fill in blanks to compare the sky to life.
- Elaborate on an idea that applies to oneself.
- Draw a personal celestial scene.
- Compose a personal inspirational message.
- Apply peers' messages to one's life.

Daring to Dare
- Explain the ways a quotation about daring to dare applies to one's life.
- Identify healthy risks one would like to take.
- Complete sentence starters about specific aspects of life in which one dares to dare.
- Present findings about Maya Angelou's other words of wisdom to peers.

The Human Touch
- Read a poem about two ways to show kindness.
- Name a close person who needs one's kindness.
- Identify ways to use these tools to impact the person's life.
- Describe how thoughtful acts will affect oneself.
- Explain ways to use these abilities with people outside one's inner circle.
- State how to help oneself by using these tools.

Coping SKILLionaire
- Take healthy risks by volunteering to ask or answer questions.
- Show humility by asking for help if needed.
- Demonstrate coping skill knowledge by responding to questions.

In the Future, My World ...

I will live in a country of my own making.
In the future,
Environmental destruction will be the norm.
No longer can it be said that
My peers and I care about this Earth.

~ Excerpt from *The Lost Generation* by Jonathan Reed

**FYI – Note how the meaning changes if you read the poem
from the bottom line up to the top line.**

Jonathan Reed has addressed the environment; consider what you are concerned about. You may already know what you have a *heart to help*, but if you need ideas, some possibilities are:

Animal advocacy	Health issues	School
Children's needs	Homeless assistance	The arts
Community	Literacy	Veterans
Cultural rights and equality	Political issues	Violence prevention
Faith-based organizations	Safety	

Now it's your turn to compose your own poem.

In the Future, My World ...

FOR THE FACILITATOR

I. Purpose
To consider socioeconomic, political, humanitarian and spiritual issues, and become aware of, and develop altruism.

II. General Comments
Teens read a poem about the environment and then write about a cause that concerns them.

III. Possible Activities
a. Before the session, place a picture of the earth into the box.
b. At the start of the session, a volunteer takes the picture out of the box and shows it to the group.
c. Ask teens what is represented (our world).
d. Ask what it means to live in one's own little world. (Care only about oneself and close associates).
e. Point out that teens in the group might have a wider view of the world – school, community, etc.
f. Distribute the *In the Future, My World ...* handout; a volunteer reads the poem aloud.
g. Prompt another volunteer to read the poem starting at the bottom line.
h. Review the list of social causes and write teens' additional ideas on the board.
i. Remind teens that their poems do not need to rhyme.
j. Allow time for completion.
k. Encourage teens to share their poems and receive peer feedback.

IV. Enrichment Activities
a. Initiate discussion about these questions; possible responses are italicized.
   - How can teens use their artistic or literary skills to promote their causes?
     Posters, postings and pictures on social media, letters to editors, petitions, etc.
   - In what other ways can a message be spread about a particular need?
     Songs, movies, television programs, documentaries, stage plays, etc. about the topic.
   - What are the pros and cons of parades and peaceful demonstrations?
     Pros – publicity, educate the community. Cons – may be difficult to organize.
   - What are some ways to raise funds?
     Sales (baked goods, rummage, etc.), services (cut lawns, wash cars, etc.). Donate the proceeds.
   - What is the value of volunteering for a charity, faith-based or public service organization?
     A natural high from helping others, make like-minded friends, work experience for a resume.
b. Prompt teens to make plans to follow through on one or more of their ideas.

My Pearls Within

Imagine you are an oyster but don't know it!
One day you open yourself up and see three pearls - your most valuable qualities.

Describe your pearls within.

1.

2.

3.

There are pearls in each of us, if only we knew how to cultivate them with ardor and persistence.

~ Sydney J. Harris

I will cultivate my pearls with enthusiasm by ...

I am determined to ...

My Pearls Within
FOR THE FACILITATOR

I. Purpose
To recognize treasures within.

II. General Comments
Teens identify their positive qualities (pearls) and learn that as irritants produce pearls, upsets can create character.

III. Possible Activities
a. Before the session, place a picture of pearls, or costume pearl jewelry, into the box.
b. At the start of the session, a volunteer takes the item out of the box and shows it to the group.
c. Pose the question "Where do pearls come from?" (oysters).
d. Ask about the process (a foreign substance or irritant enters the shell; layers of coating form a pearl).
e. Distribute the *My Pearls Within* handout; a volunteer reads the directions aloud.
f. Emphasize that teens are to elaborate on each quality.
g. Allow time for completion.
h. Encourage teens to share their responses and receive peer feedback.

Possibilities
- My most valuable qualities are…

Academic ability	Hope	Musical talent
Athleticism	Gratitude	Open-mindedness
Artistic talent	Honesty	Originality
Courage	Humility	Resilience
Creativity	Individualism	Self-discipline
Curiosity	Kindness	Verbal and written skills
Empathy	Leadership	
Faith	Loyalty	

Elaborations will be individualized.
- I will cultivate my *pearls* with enthusiasm by …
  Reminding myself to use them, even when it's difficult.
  Sharpening my skills through practice.
- I am determined to …
  Generate new *pearls*.
  Let no one or nothing stop me.

IV. Enrichment Activities
Ask, "If an irritant helps create a pearl, how can a problem bring out your best qualities?"

Possibilities
- Music, art, and writing talent are portrayed through a wide range of situations and emotions.
- Courage, faith and hope often emerge out of necessity in adversity.
- Honesty, open-mindedness and kindness are put to the test during opportunities to be dishonest, bigoted and cruel.

Night Sky Inspirations

Think how the night sky might inspire you.

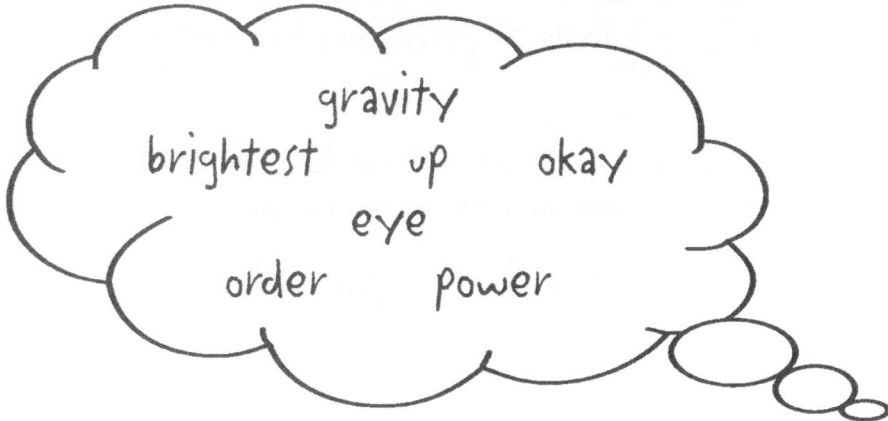

gravity
brightest   up   okay
eye
order   power

Use the thought cloud to fill in the blanks.

There is a _____ beyond this world.

There is _____ to the universe.

I must look _____ to see the beauty.

Stars are _____ when it is darkest.

I don't know everything and that's _____.

The astronaut said, *Don't let* _____ *hold you down.*

The crescent moon said, *There's more to me than meets the* _____.

Place a star in front of an idea that applies to your life. Elaborate below.

_____

_____

Draw your celestial scene (star, moon, comet, constellation, etc.) and write
its inspirational message.

Night Sky Inspirations

FOR THE FACILITATOR

I. Purpose
To see the night sky as a source of inspiration.

II. General Comments
In other sessions teens tap into inner treasures; in this activity teens focus on wisdom outside themselves.

III. Possible Activities
a. Before the session, place a picture of stars in the night sky, into the box.
b. At the start of the session, a volunteer takes the picture out of the box and shows it to the group.
c. Encourage discussion among teens who have looked through telescopes or visited planetariums, etc.
d. Distribute the *Night Sky Inspirations* handout; a volunteer reads the directions aloud.
e. Allow time for completion.
f. Encourage teens to share their responses.
   Possibilities
   - Fill in the blanks: power, order, up, brightest, okay, gravity, eye.
   - Ways the sentences may apply to teens' lives :
     There is a power beyond this world inspires teens contemplate their spirituality; to have faith.
        There is order to the universe urges teens believe they can be calm in chaos; to have peace.
     I must look up to see beauty encourages teens to choose an upbeat outlook; to be optimistic.
     Stars are brightest when it is darkest helps teens have hope in adversity; to recognize light bulb moments.
     I don't know everything and that's ok reminds teens that life holds mysteries; to accept uncertainty.
     Don't let gravity hold you down shows teens that negative forces can be conquered; to be determined.
     There's more to me than meets the eye prompts teens to look at inner traits; to seek authenticity.
   - Celestial scenes and their inspirational messages will be individual expressions.

IV. Enrichment Exercises
a. Suggest that teens cut out the boxes in which they drew and wrote.
b. The cutouts remain anonymous.
c. A volunteer collects the cutouts and scrambles them.
d. Teens take turns picking peers' cutouts from the pile and sharing with the group how the messages apply to their own lives.

Daring to Dare

I believe that the most important single thing, beyond discipline and creativity, is daring to dare.

~ Maya Angelou

Example: I dare my eyes to see ...
my own strengths and weaknesses.

I dare my eyes to see ...

I dare my ears to hear ...

I dare my mind to think ...

I dare my lips to speak ...

I dare my hands to do this work ...

I dare my feet to go ...

I dare my heart to feel ...

I dare myself to be ...

I dare myself to become ...

Daring to Dare

FOR THE FACILITATOR

I. Purpose
To take healthy risks, to expand perceptions and expectations.

II. General Comments
Cowardice and fear may keep teens from recognizing truths, feeling emotions and daring to become more than they thought they could be.

III. Possible Activities
a. Before the session, place a picture of Maya Angelou into the box.
b. At the start of the session, a volunteer takes the picture out of the box and shows it to the group.
c. Ask teens about Ms. Angelou's identity (famous author, poet, performer, director, etc.).
d. Write "Dare" on the board and ask its meaning (teens may say "to defy or provoke" but elicit its other meaning – "to have the courage or to risk" e.g., "Dare to be different.")
e. Distribute the *Daring to Dare* handout; ask teens the title's meaning (having courage to face a challenge).
f. A volunteer reads the quotation aloud.
g. Allow time for completion.
h. Encourage teens to share their responses and receive peer feedback.
   Possibilities
   I Dare to …
   *   *See* my own strengths and weaknesses, the truth about people who may have a negative influence on me, the reality of a situation I have denied, etc.
   *   *Hear* constructive criticism, the falsity of lies I would rather believe, helpful new information, what others think and feel, etc.
   *   *Think* about the possibilities in every problem, about others in my circle and beyond, about my current life, goals and future.
   *   *Speak* my beliefs, values and ambitions in the presence of opposition, my truth as gently as possible when necessary and speak up for others who are mistreated or do not use their voice.
   *   *Do this work* – my passion e.g. draw, paint, sculpt, write, sing, dance, teach, fix mechanical objects, fight for my country, raise a family, etc.; my disliked temporary job to meet my financial needs while in school; to help others when it's inconvenient but important, etc.
   *   *Go* – to people with whom I need to make amends, to places that will benefit me physically, emotionally, spiritually; to places that seem scary but challenge me to meet goals; to locations where I will be a blessing to others, etc.
   *   *Feel* – pain if necessary for growth; compassion, enthusiasm; disappointment but deal with it, etc.
   *   *Be* – myself, but my best self, a work in progress, disciplined, creative, caring and daring.
   *   *Become* – more than I had thought I could become; a person who makes a difference, etc.

IV. Enrichment Activities
a. Encourage teens individually or in teams to research Maya Angelou's biography, read her quotations, poems and books, and to explore her other works.
b. Suggest that teens give presentations to peers about their findings.

THE HUMAN TOUCH

'Tis the human touch in this world that counts,
The touch of your hand and mine,
Which means far more to the fainting heart
Than shelter and bread and wine.
For shelter is gone when the night is o'er,
And bread lasts only a day,
But the touch of the hand
And the sound of the voice
Sing on in the soul always.

~ Spencer Michael Free

Who in your inner circle of family and friends needs your kind touch and the sound of your voice?

_____

_____

By doing this, how will you have an effect and make a difference to this person?

_____

_____

By doing this, how will it have an effect on you?

_____

_____

What words will "sing on in the person's soul"?

_____

_____

THE HUMAN TOUCH
FOR THE FACILITATOR

I. Purpose
To recognize the potential in one's hands and voice.

II. General Comments
Teens recognize two tools to show they care and identify ways to use them.

III. Possible Activities
a. Before the session, on a piece of paper, place an outline of a hand into the box.
b. At the start of the session, a volunteer takes the paper out of the box and shows it to the group.
c. Explain that teens will read a poem about the touch of a hand.
  • Elicit the many types of touch – a clasp of friendship, a handshake to seal a deal, a pat on the back, healing touch (backrub or massage).
  • Teens may mention sexual touch; acknowledge that touch plays a part in romance and sexuality but this topic is about other types of touch.
d. Distribute the *The Human Touch* handout.
e. A volunteer reads the poem aloud.
f. Allow time for completion.
g. Encourage teens to share their responses and receive peer feedback.
  Possibilities
  • Persons who need teens' touch and voice may be relatives, friends, lonely or sick people.
  • The effect and difference to the person may be to know they are loved, that the teen cares, and to be encouraged; it could make their life worth living.
  • The effect on the teens would be satisfaction and self-respect knowing that their hands and voice brightened someone's day or improved their life.
  • Words that sing on in souls may be "I love you … You can do it… You were right …," etc.
h. Encourage teens to brainstorm other ways to use their hands to help.
  Possibilities
  • Volunteer to hold babies, or the hands of people who are elderly or sick at facilities.
  • Shake patients' hands while volunteering at a veteran's hospital.
i. Encourage teens to brainstorm other ways to use their voices to help.
  Possibilities
  • Read to children at a library; share an issue close to one's heart in assemblies, at meetings, etc.
  • Read poetry and inspirational passages to a person who is bed-bound or needs to be uplifted.

IV. Enrichment Activities
a. Ask teens how their voices and hands are gifts to themselves.
  Possibilities
  Teens can use their hands to:
  • Express themselves creatively through art, writing, computer graphics, mechanics, etc.
  • Play an instrument, work at any job that fulfills a passion or meets financial needs.
  Teens can use their voices to:
  • Say "Yes" to positives, "No" to negatives, stand up for themselves and others.
  • Sing; speak words of faith at a house of worship, read encouraging passages aloud to themselves.
b. Suggest that teens draw a large hand on poster paper and tape it to the wall.
  • Teens use their writers' voices to pen encouraging words on the hand.
  • Display the poster where teens from other classes or groups can add to it; all who view the hand will benefit from its messages.

Coping SKILLionaire

Instructions for Game Show Host

Game Show Host writes the game title and categories on the board before the game:

Who Wants to Be a SKILLionaire?
Coping Categories:

De-Stress   Empowerment   Habits   Media
Stand Up   Overcome   Thrive

Game Show Host explains:

"In this game everyone who attempts to answer is a *SKILLionaire*.
Players can ask the group for assistance.
To play, raise your hand and pick a category.
I'll read a question and two possible replies; you choose the best response.
Let's play … Who Wants to Be a SKILLionaire!"

DIS-STRESS

1. In a stressful situation is it helpful to …
    a. Magnify the problem
    b. See the whole picture
2. What would a surfer say?
    a. "Feel the fear and enjoy the ride."
    b. "Get off the board and walk to your destination."
3. You want revenge. Which is the better action to take?
    a. Do what you want to do.
    b. In an assertive way, tell the person how you feel.
4. Regarding someone's opinions of you, tell yourself …
    a. "What that person thinks is not my problem."
    b. "I'm bothered by what that person might think."
5. Vicious rumors about you have gone viral.
    a. Know that people who spread them have their own problems.
    b. Spread worse words about the perpetrators.
6. You are totally stressed out.
    a. Worry and wallow in misery.
    b. Do something productive.
7. You need help with a crisis in your life.
    a. Turn to drugs or alcohol.
    b. Ask a trusted adult for advice.

(Continued on the next page)

Coping SKILLionaire *(Continued)*

EMPOWERMENT

8. In the heat of anger …
    a. Explode with hurtful words.
    b. Chill, think, and act assertively.
9. What's your opinion of hate crimes?
    a. They're here to stay.
    b. Hate can be un-learned.
10. Which is the better way to handle fear?
    a. Face it.
    b. Hide from it.
11. Which describes perseverance?
    a. Stick to it.
    b. Give up.
12. When is the time to be selfish?
    a. Never.
    b. Sometimes.
13. Your feelings are hurt. What do you do?
    a. Give the person power to cause you pain.
    b. Take charge of your own thoughts and feelings.
14. Someone tries to talk you into something you know could be harmful. What do you do?
    a. Do it or else that person won't be your friend.
    b. Know that a good friend wouldn't pressure you to do something harmful.
15. Which has more influence over you?
    a. What others say.
    b. What you say to yourself.
16. Which do you think is worse?
    a. To care about nothing.
    b. To care too much.

HABITS

17. What makes it easier to give up an unhealthy habit?
    a. Think about the consequences.
    b. Focus on the rewards of the healthier habits.
18. Which is a more positive outlook?
    a. People are like tigers that never change their stripes.
    b. People are like caterpillars that can become butterflies.
19. How do you launch a new positive habit?
    a. Reminders, repetition and rewards.
    b. Give up if you are unsuccessful.
20. When you reach a short-term goal …
    a. Decide it is good enough.
    b. Energize for the next step.

MEDIA

21. When it comes to many online profiles …
    a. Seeing is believing.
    b. Looks are deceiving.
22. If your online profile is authentic …
    a. What people see is what they get.
    b. They don't see the real deal.
23. Which provides more support?
    a. Lots of online friends you rarely see face-to-face.
    b. A few friends who are up close and personal.
24. To truly influence people, tell them to …
    a. "Do as I say."
    b. "Do as I do."

(Continued on the next page)

Coping SKILLionaire *(Continued)*

STAND UP

25. As a bystander you observe bullying. Know that …
    a. It's best to do nothing because it's none of your business.
    b. Tell a trusted adult (anonymously if necessary).
26. Which is true?
    a. Cruelty is cowardice.
    b. Cruelty is courageous.
27. A friend asks you to do a favor you really do not want to do. To be assertive, you…
    a. Say "No" and stick to it.
    b. Say "Yes" then make an excuse at the last minute.
28. When people put you down, which is better …
    a. Let them keep you down.
    b. Realize they are lower down.
29. Which is true?
    a. People who bully, are bullies.
    b. People who bully, are people who bully.

OVERCOME

30. You have a dilemma. Someone suggests a mind map. Your open-minded response …
    a. "I don't need one; I have it all in my head."
    b. "It might help me see all of my options."
31. When it comes to unpleasant circumstances, which is the more helpful motto?
    a. "Look for the message in the mess."
    b. "Rant, rave and run!"
32. You want to enter the try-outs but the competition is tough. You are better off to …
    a. Decide not to try because you might not make it.
    b. Do your best and enjoy the experience.

OVERCOME *(continued)*

33. Which philosophy is more productive?
    a. Wait for the rainbow.
    b. Learn to love the rain.
34. In troubling times which makes sense?
    a. Find strength in oneself, supportive people and spirituality.
    b. Accept victimhood.

THRIVE

35. An important part of thriving is to …
    a. Be rich, famous and good looking.
    b. Care about a cause outside yourself.
36. You have unrecognized potential. To access it you …
    a. Reach into your heart and pull it out.
    b. Wait for someone to discover it.
37. On a clear night you look at the sky. Which is better to think?
    a. I play an important role in an amazing universe.
    b. I am scared of the unknown.
38. You dare yourself to face a challenge and you flop. Dare to decide …
    a. "I'll never go through that pain again."
    b. "I'll try again."
39. Your best friend is going through a break up. As a supportive person you …
    a. Decide it's enough to text your sympathy because it's quick and convenient.
    b. Provide face-to-face comfort after you text.
40. What new thought do you want to keep in mind as you live your life?
    (Accept any positive individual responses).

Coping SKILLionaire

FOR THE FACILITATOR

I. Purpose
To review and reinforce skills developed in previous sessions.

II. General Comments
Through a simulated game show and as a non-threatening review tool, teens recall lessons learned.

III. Possible Activities
a. Before the session, write "$1,000,000.00" in large print on a piece of paper and place it into the box.
b. Before the session, decide whether to use the Game Show Format or the Recap Format below and make the indicated number of photocopies.
c. At the start of the session, a volunteer takes the paper out of the box and shows it to the group.
d. Ask teens how they would spend a million dollars (individual responses).

Game Show Format
- Make one photocopy of each page of the *Coping SKILLionaire* handout (pages 111, 112, 113).
- Make one copy of this facilitator's page because it has the answer key for the host.
- Explain that teens will play a game to reinforce some recently addressed concepts.
- Recruit a volunteer who is comfortable reading aloud to play the host.
- Give the host a photocopy of the *Coping SKILLionaire* handout pages plus the facilitator's page.
- The host writes the game show title and categories on the board.
- Volunteers take turns choosing categories and responding to the questions read by the host.
- The host crosses off each question as it is used and asks only new questions in each category.
- The host uses the answer key below to verify correct responses.
- Answers are meant to be easy; the purpose is to reinforce, not test the teens.

Recap Format
- Distribute one photocopy of the *Coping SKILLionaire* handout (pages 111, 112, 113) per participant.
- Advise them to disregard the Game Show Instructions and focus on the forty questions.
- Teens are to circle the letter for each correct response.
- Allow time for completion.
- Review and discuss the correct answers.

Answer Key

1 – b	2 – a	3 – b	4 – a	5 – a	6 – b	7 – b	8 – b	9 – b	10 – a
11 – a	12 – b	13 – b	14 – b	15 – b	16 – a	17 – b	18 – b	19 – a	20 – b
21 – b	22 – a	23 – b	24 – b	25 – b	26 – a	27 – a	28 – b	29 – b	30 – b
31 – a	32 – b	33 – b	34 – a	35 – b	36 – a	37 – a	38 – b	39 – b	40 – N/A

IV. Enrichment Activities
a. Encourage all teens to respond to item number 40 and receive peer feedback.
b. Invite teens to share their ideas for future *out-of-the-box coping skills* sessions.

wholeperson

Whole Person Associates is the leading publisher of training resources for professionals who empower people to create and maintain healthy lifestyles. Our creative resources will help you work effectively with your clients in the areas of stress management, wellness promotion, mental health and life skills.

Please visit us at our web site: **www.wholeperson. com**. You can check out our entire line of products, place an order, request our print catalog, and sign up for our monthly special notifications.

Whole Person Associates
800-247-6789